THE DEVACHANIC PLANE

OR

THE HEAVEN WORLD

ITS CHARACTERISTICS AND INHABITANTS

BY

Charles Webster Leadbeater

"THE ASTRAL PLANE," "CLAIRVOYANCE,"
"THE CHRISTIAN CREED," ETC., ETC.

A Yesterday's World Publishing

Published by A Yesterday's World Publishing
Copyright © 2019 A Yesterday's World Publishing
First impression 2019
ISBN - 978-1-912925-56-8

CONTENTS

PREFACE.

Few words are needed in sending this little book out into the world. It is the sixth of a series of Manuals designed to meet the public demand for a simple exposition of Theosophical teachings. Some have complained that our literature is at once too abstruse, too technical, and too expensive for the ordinary reader, and it is our hope that the present series may succeed in supplying what is a very real want. Theosophy is not only for the learned; it is for all. Perhaps among those who in these little books catch their first glimpse of its teachings, there may be a few who will be led by them to penetrate more deeply into its philosophy, its science and its religion, facing its abstruser problems with the student's zeal and the neophyte's ardour. But these Manuals are not written for the eager student, whom no initial difficulties can daunt; they are written for the busy men and women of the work-a-day world, and seek to make plain some of the great truths that render life easier to bear and death easier to face. Written by servants of the Masters who are the Elder Brothers of our race, they can have no other object than to serve our fellow-men.

INTRODUCTION.

IN the introduction to the manual recently issued on *The Astral Plane, I* remarked that "a good deal of information on the subject of this realm of nature is to be found scattered here and there in our books, but there is not, so far as I am aware, any single volume to which one can turn for a complete summary of the facts at present known to us about this interesting region." It seems evident that this remark applies with even greater force to the plane next above the astral—that of Devachan or Sukhâvatî. There is indeed a most instructive chapter on the subject in that indispensable text-book of every Theosophical student, Mr. Sinnett's *Esoteric Buddhism;* but though nothing which we have since learnt has in any way contradicted the lucid exposition of the devachanic state there given, it is nevertheless true that such investigations as we have been able to make during the thirteen years which have elapsed since it was written have placed us in possession of a considerable body of additional information as to details. It will be readily understood that there are many minor points about which Mr. Sinnett could not venture to trouble his Adept correspondent, which are nevertheless of the greatest interest to humanity, since by far the greater part of its existence is passed upon the plane under consideration—a plane which is in fact the true and permanent home of the reincarnating ego, each descent into incarnation being merely a short though all-important episode in its career. The object of this manual then is to present a summary of the facts about Devachan at present known to us; and, as previously in the case of the astral plane, I am requested by our investigators to say that, while they deprecate the ascription of anything like authority to their statements, they have felt it due to their fellow-students to take every precaution in their power to ensure accuracy. Indeed, I may say that in this case also "no fact, old or new, has been admitted to this treatise unless it has been confirmed by the testimony of at least two independent trained investigators among ourselves, and has also been passed as correct by older students whose knowledge on these points is necessarily much greater than ours. It is hoped therefore that this account, though it cannot be considered as complete, may yet be found reliable as far as it goes."

I will not here reproduce the remarks made in the previous manual as to the absolute necessity, to the student of Occultism, of a definite realization of the fact that nature is divided into various great planes, each with its own matter of different degrees of density, and each interpenetrating those below it—though these observations are quite as applicable to the study of the devachanic plane as to the astral: I will simply refer the enquirer on that matter to the introduction to Theosophical Manual No. V., and recapitulate here only so far as to remind the reader that Devachan is the third of the five great planes with which humanity is at present concerned, having below it the astral and the physical, and above it the buddhic (sometimes, though perhaps less appropriately, called the sushuptic) and the nirvânic. As just now remarked, it is the plane upon which man, unless at an exceedingly early stage of his progress, spends by far the greater part of his time during the process of evolution; for, except in the case of the entirely undeveloped, the proportion of the physical life to the devachanic is rarely much greater than one in twenty, and in the case of fairly good people it would sometimes fall as low as one in forty. It is therefore well worth our while to devote to its study such time and care as may be necessary to acquire as thorough a comprehension of it as is possible for us while encased in the physical body.

Unfortunately there are practically insuperable difficulties in the way of any attempt to put the facts of this third plane of nature into language—and not unnaturally, for we often find words insufficient to express our ideas and feelings even on this lowest plane. Readers of *The Astral Plane* will remember what was there stated as to the impossibility of conveying any adequate conception of the marvels of that region to those whose experience had not as yet transcended the physical world; one can but say that every observation there made to that effect applies with tenfold force to the effort which is before us in this sequel to that treatise. Not only is the matter which we must endeavour to describe much further removed than is astral matter from that to which we are accustomed, but the consciousness of that plane is so immensely wider than anything we can imagine down here, and its very conditions so entirely different, that when called upon to translate it all into mere ordinary words the explorer feels himself utterly at a loss, and can only trust that the intuition of his readers will supplement the inevitable imperfections of his description.

To take one only out of many possible examples, it would seem as though in Devachan space and time were non-existent, for events which here take place in succession and at widely-separated places, appear there to be occurring simultaneously and at the same point. That at least is the effect produced on the consciousness of the ego, though there are circumstances which favour the supposition that absolute simultaneity is the attribute of a still higher plane, and that the sensation of it in Devachan is simply the result of a succession so rapid that the infinitesimally minute spaces of time are indistinguishable, just as, in the well-known optical experiment of whirling round a stick the end of which is red-hot, the eye receives the impression of a continuous ring of fire if the stick be whirled more than ten times a second; not because a continuous ring really exists, but because the average human eye is incapable of distinguishing as separate any similar impressions which follow one another at intervals of less than the tenth part of a second.

However that may be, the reader will readily comprehend that in the endeavour to describe a condition of existence so totally unlike that of physical life as is the one which we have to consider, it will be impossible to avoid saying many things that will be partly unintelligible and may even seem wholly incredible to those who have not personally experienced the devachanic life. That this should he so is, as I have said, quite inevitable, so readers who find themselves unable to accept the report of our investigators must simply wait for a more satisfactory account of Devachan until they are able to examine it for themselves: I can only repeat the assurance that all reasonable precautions have been taken to ensure accuracy.

The general arrangement of the previous manual will as far as possible be followed in this one also, so that those who wish to do so will be able to compare the two planes stage by stage. The heading "Scenery" would however be inappropriate to Devachan, as will be seen later; we will therefore substitute for it the title which follows.

GENERAL CHARACTERISTICS.

Perhaps the least unsatisfactory method of approaching this exceedingly difficult subject will be to plunge *in medias res* and make the attempt (foredoomed to failure though it be) to depict what a pupil sees when first the devachanic plane opens before him. I use the word pupil advisedly, for unless a man stand in that relation to a qualified Master, there is but little likelihood of his being able to pass in full consciousness into that glorious land of bliss, and return to earth with clear remembrance of that which he has seen there. Thence no accommodating "spirit" ever comes to utter cheap platitudes through the mouth of the professional medium; thither no ordinary clairvoyant ever rises, though sometimes the best and purest have entered it when in deepest trance they slipped from the control of their Mesmerizers—yet even then they have rarely brought back more than a faint recollection of an intense but indescribable bliss, generally deeply coloured by their personal religious convictions.

When once the departed ego, withdrawing into himself after what we call death, has reached that plane, neither the yearning thoughts of his sorrowing friends nor the allurements of the spiritualistic circle can ever draw him back into communion with the physical earth until all the spiritual forces which he has set in motion in his recent life have worked themselves out to the full, and he once more stands ready to take upon himself new robes of flesh. Nor, even if he could so return, would his account of his experiences give any true idea of the plane, for, as will presently be, seen, it is only those who can enter it in full waking consciousness who are able to move about freely and drink in all the wondrous glory and beauty which Devachan has to show. But all this will be more fully explained later, when we come to deal with the inhabitants of this celestial realm.

A BEAUTIFUL DESCRIPTION.

In an early letter from an eminent occultist the following beautiful passage was given as a quotation from memory. I have never been able to discover whence it was taken, though what seems to be another version of it, considerably expanded, appears in Beal's *Catena of Buddhist Scriptures*, p. 378.

"Our Lord BUDDHA says: Many thousand myriads of systems of worlds beyond this is a region of bliss called Sukhâvatî. This region is encircled within seven rows of railings, seven rows of vast curtains, seven rows of waving trees. This holy abode of the Arhats is governed by the Tathâgatas and is possessed by the Bodhisattvas. It has seven precious lakes, in the midst of which flow crystalline waters having seven and yet one distinctive properties and qualities. This, O Sâriputra, is the Devachan. Its divine udambara flower casts a root in the shadow of every earth, and blossoms for all those who reach it. Those born in this blessed region—who have crossed the golden bridge and reached the seven golden mountains—they are truly felicitous; there is no more grief or sorrow in that cycle for them."

Veiled though they be under the gorgeous imagery of the Orient, we may easily trace in this passage some of the leading characteristics which have appeared most prominently in the accounts of our own modern investigators. The "seven golden mountains" can be but the seven subdivisions of the devachanic plane, separated from one another by barriers impalpable, yet real and effective there as "seven rows of railings, seven rows of vast curtains, seven rows of waving trees" might be here: the seven kinds of crystalline water, having each its distinctive properties and

3

qualities, represent the different powers and conditions of mind belonging to them respectively, while the one quality which they all have in common is that of ensuring to those residing upon them the utmost intensity of bliss which they are capable of experiencing. Its flower indeed "casts a root in the shadow of every earth," for from every world man enters the corresponding Devachan, and happiness such as no tongue may tell is the blossom which burgeons forth for all who so live as to fit themselves to attain it. For they have "crossed the golden bridge" over the stream which divides this realm from Kâmaloka; for them the struggle between the higher and the lower is over, and for them, therefore, is "no more grief or sorrow in that cycle," until once more the ego puts himself forth into incarnation, and the celestial world is again left for a time behind.

THE BLISS OF DEVACHAN.

This intensity of bliss is the first great idea which must form a background to all our conceptions of Devachan. It is not only that we are dealing with a world in which, by its very constitution, evil and sorrow are impossible; it is not only a world in which every creature is happy: the facts of the case go far beyond all that. It is a world in which every being must, from the very fact of his presence there, be enjoying the highest spiritual bliss of which he is capable—a world whose power of response to his aspirations is limited only by his capacity to aspire. How this can be so we must endeavour to make clear later on; the point to be emphasized for the moment is that this radiant sense not only of the welcome absence of all evil and discord, but of the insistent, over-whelming presence of universal joy, is the first and most striking sensation experienced by him who enters upon the devachanic plane. And it never leaves him so long as he remains there; whatever work he may be doing, whatever still higher possibilities of spiritual exaltation may arise before him as he learns more of the capabilities of this new world in which he finds himself, the strange indescribable feeling of inexpressible delight in mere existence in such a realm underlies all else—this enjoyment of the abounding joy of others is ever present with him. Nothing on earth is like it, nothing can image it; if one could suppose the bounding life of childhood carried up into our spiritual experience and then intensified many thousandfold, perhaps some faint shadow of an idea of it might be suggested; yet even such a simile falls miserably short of that which lies beyond all words—the tremendous spiritual vitality of the devachanic plane.

One way in which this intense vitality manifests itself is the extreme rapidity of vibration of all particles and atoms of devachanic matter. As a theoretical proposition we are all aware that even here on the physical plane no particle of matter, though forming part of the densest of solid bodies, is ever for a moment at rest; nevertheless when by the opening of astral vision this becomes for us no longer a mere theory of the scientists, but an actual and ever-present fact, we realize the universality of life in a manner and to an extent that was quite impossible before; our mental horizon widens out and we begin even already to have glimpses of possibilities in nature which to those who cannot yet see must appear the wildest of dreams.

If this be the effect of acquiring the mere astral vision, and applying it to dense physical matter, try to imagine the result produced on the mind of the observer when, having left this lower plane behind and thoroughly studied the far more vivid life and infinitely more rapid vibrations of Kâmaloka, he finds a new and transcendent sense opening within him, which unfolds to his enraptured gaze yet another and a higher world, whose vibrations are as much quicker than those of our physical plane as vibrations of light are than those of sound—a world where the omnipresent life which pulsates ceaselessly around and within him is of a different order altogether, is as it were raised to an enormously higher power.

THE DEVACHANIC SENSE.

The very sense itself, by which he is enabled to cognize all this, is not the least of the marvels of this celestial world; no longer does he hear and see and feel by separate and limited organs, as he does down here, nor has he even the immensely extended capacity of sight and hearing which he possessed on the astral plane; instead of these he feels within him a strange new power which is not any of them, and yet includes them all and much more—a power which enables him the moment any person or thing comes before him not only to see it and feel it and hear it, but to know all about it instantly inside and out—its causes, its effects, and its possibilities, so far at least as that plane and all below it are concerned. He finds that for him to think is to realize; there is never any doubt, hesitation, or delay, about this direct action of the higher sense. If he thinks of a place, he is there; if of a friend, that friend is before him. No longer can misunderstandings arise, no longer can he be deceived or misled by any outward appearances, for every thought and feeling of his friend lies open as a book before him on that plane.

And if he is fortunate enough to have among his friends another whose higher sense is opened, their intercourse is perfect beyond all earthly conception. For them distance and separation do not exist; their feelings are no longer hidden or at best but half expressed by clumsy words; question and answer are unnecessary, for the thought-pictures are read as they are formed, and the interchange of ideas is as rapid as is their flashing into existence in the mind.

All knowledge is theirs for the searching—all, that is, which does not transcend even this lofty plane; the past of the world is as open to them as the present; the âkâshic records are ever at their disposal, and history, whether ancient or modern, unfolds itself before their eyes at their will. No longer are they at the mercy of the historian, who may be ill-informed, and must be more or less partial; they can study for themselves any incident in which they are interested, with the absolute certainty of seeing "the truth, the whole truth, and nothing but the truth." If they are able to stand upon the higher or arûpa levels of the plane the long line of their past lives unrolls itself before them like a scroll; they see the karmic causes which have made them what they are; they see what Karma still lies in front to be worked out before "the long sad count is closed," and thus they realize with unerring certainty their exact place in evolution.

If it be asked whether they can see the future clearly as the past, the answer must be in the negative, for though prevision is to a great extent possible to them, yet it is not perfect, because wherever in the web of destiny the hand of the developed man comes in, his powerful will may introduce new threads, and change the pattern of the life to come. The course of the ordinary undeveloped man, who has practically no will of his own worth speaking of, may often be foreseen clearly enough, but when the ego boldly takes his future into his own hands, exact prevision becomes impossible.

SURROUNDINGS.

The first impressions, then, of the pupil who enters the devachanic plane in full consciousness will probably be those of intense bliss, indescribable vitality, and enormously increased power. And when he makes use of his new sense to examine his surroundings, what does he see? He finds himself in the midst of what seems to him a whole universe of ever-changing light and colour and sound, such as it has never entered into his loftiest dreams to imagine. Verily it is true that down here "eye hath not seen, nor ear hath heard, neither hath it entered into the heart of man to conceive" the glories of the devachanic plane: and the man who has once experienced them in full consciousness will regard the world with widely different eyes for ever after. Yet this experience is so utterly unlike anything we know on the physical plane that in trying to put it into words one is troubled by a curious sense of helplessness—of absolute incapacity, not only to do it justice, for of *that* one resigns all hope from the very outset, but even to give any idea at all of it to those who have not themselves seen it.

Let a man imagine himself, with the feelings of intense bliss and enormously increased power already described, floating in a sea of living light, surrounded by every conceivable variety of loveliness in colour and form—the whole changing with every wave of thought that he sends out from his mind, and being indeed, as he presently discovers, only the expression of his thought in the matter of the plane and in its elemental essence. For that matter is of the very same order as that of which the mind-body is itself composed, and therefore when that vibration of the particles of the mind-body which we call a thought occurs, it immediately extends itself to this surrounding devachanic matter, and sets up corresponding vibrations in it, while in the elemental essence it images itself with absolute exactitude. Concrete thought naturally takes the shape of its objects, while abstract ideas usually represent themselves by all kinds of perfect and most beautiful geometrical forms; though in this connection it should be remembered that many thoughts which are little more than the merest abstractions to us down here become concrete facts on this loftier plane.

It will thus be seen that in Devachan anyone who wishes to devote himself for a time to quiet thought, and to abstract himself from his surroundings, may actually live in a world of his own without possibility of interruption, and with the additional advantage of seeing all his ideas and their consequences fully worked out passing in a sort of panorama before his eyes. If, however, he wishes instead to observe the plane upon which he finds himself, it will be necessary for him very carefully to suspend his thought for the time, so that its creations may not influence the readily impressible matter around him, and thus alter the entire conditions so far as he is concerned.

This holding of the mind in suspense must not be confounded with the blankness of mind towards the attainment of which so many of the Hatha Yoga practices are directed: in the latter case the mind is dulled down into absolute passivity in order that it may not by any thought of its own offer resistance to the entry of any external influence that may happen to approach it—a condition closely approximating to medium-ship; while in the former the mind is as keenly alert and positive as it can be, holding its thought in suspense for the moment merely to prevent the intrusion of a personal equation into the observation which it wishes to make.

When the visitor to the devachanic plane succeeds in putting himself in this position he finds that although he is no longer himself a centre of radiation of all that marvellous wealth of light and colour, form and sound, which I have so vainly endeavoured to picture, it has not therefore ceased to exist; on the contrary, its harmonies and its coruscations are but grander and fuller than ever. Casting about for an explanation of this phenomenon, he begins to realize that all this magnificence is not a mere idle or fortuitous display —a kind of devachanic aurora borealis; he finds that it all has a meaning—a meaning which he himself can understand; and presently he grasps the fact that what he is watching with such ecstasy of delight is simply the glorious colour-language of the Devas—the expression of the thought or the conversation of beings far higher than himself in the scale of evolution. By experiment and practice he discovers that he also can use this new and beautiful mode of expression, and by this very discovery he enters into possession of another great tract of his heritage in this celestial realm—the power to hold converse with, and to learn from, its loftier non-human inhabitants, with whom we shall deal more fully when we come to treat of that part of our subject.

By this time it will have become apparent why it was impossible to devote a section of this paper to the scenery of Devachan, as was done in the case of the astral plane; for in point of fact Devachan has *no* scenery except such as each individual chooses to make for himself by his thought—unless indeed we take into account the fact that the vast numbers of entities who are continually passing before him are themselves objects in many cases of the most transcendent beauty.

THE GREAT WAVES.

If the visitor wishes to carry his analysis of the plane still further, and discover what it would be when entirely undisturbed by the thought or conversation of any of its, inhabitants, he can do so by forming round himself a huge shell through which none of these influences can penetrate, and then (of course holding his own mind perfectly still as before) examining the conditions which exist inside his shell.

If he performs this experiment with sufficient care, he will find that the sea of light has become—not still, for its particles continue their intense and rapid vibration, but as it were homogeneous; that those wonderful coruscations of colour and constant changes of form are no longer taking place, but that he is now able to perceive another and entirely different series of regular pulsations which the other more artificial phenomena had previously obscured. These are evidently universal, and no shell which human power can make will check or turn them aside. They cause no change of colour, no assumption of form, but flow with resistless regularity through all the matter of the plane, outwards and in again, like the exhalations and inhalations of some great breath beyond our ken.

There are several sets of these, clearly distinguishable from one another by volume and by period of vibration, and grander than them all sweeps one great wave which seems the very heart-beat of the system—a wave which, welling up from unknown centres on far higher planes, pours out its life through all our world, and then draws back in its tremendous tide to That from which it came. In one long undulating curve it comes, and the sound of it is like the murmur of the sea; and yet in it and through it all the while there echoes a mighty ringing chant of triumph—the very music of the spheres. The man who once has heard that glorious song of nature never quite loses it again; even here on this dreary physical plane of illusion he hears it always as a kind of undertone, keeping ever before his mind the strength and light and splendour of the real life above.

If the visitor be pure in heart and mind, and has reached a certain degree of spiritual development, it is possible for him to identify his consciousness with the sweep of that wondrous wave—to merge his spirit in it, as it were, and let it bear him upward to its source. It is possible, I say; but it is not wise—unless, indeed, his Master stands beside him to draw him back at the right moment from its mighty embrace; for otherwise its irresistible force will carry him away onward and upward into still higher planes, whose far greater glories his ego is as yet unable to sustain; he will lose consciousness, and with no certainty as to when and where and how he will regain it. It is true that the ultimate object of man's evolution is the attainment of unity, but he must reach that final goal in full and perfect consciousness as a victorious king entering triumphantly upon his heritage, not drift into absorption in a state of blank unconsciousness but little removed from annihilation.

THE RÛPA AND ARÛBA PLANES.

All that we have hitherto attempted to indicate in this description may be taken as applying to the lowest-subdivision of the devachanic plane; for this realm of nature, exactly like the astral or the physical, has its seven subdivisions. Of these four are called in the books the rûpa planes, while the other three are spoken of as arûpa or formless—the reason for these names being that on the rûpa planes every thought takes to itself a certain definite form, while on the arf.ipa subdivisions it expresses itself in an entirely different manner, as will presently be explained. The distinction between these two great divisions of the plane—the rûpa and the arûpa—is very marked; indeed, it even extends so far as to necessitate the use of different vehicles of consciousness.

The vehicle appropriate to the four rûpa levels is the mind-body, out of the matter of which the Adept forms his Mâyâvirûpa, while that of the three arûpa levels is the causal body—the vehicle of the reincarnating ego, in which he passes from life to life throughout the whole manvantara. Another enormous distinction is that on those four lower subdivisions illusion is still possible—not indeed for the entity who stands upon them in full consciousness during life, but for the person who passes there after the change which men call death. The higher thoughts and aspirations which he has poured forth during earth-life then cluster round him, and make a sort of shell about him—a kind of subjective world of his own; and in that he lives his devachanic life, seeing but very faintly or not at all the real glories of the plane which lie outside. On the three arûpa subdivisions no such self-deception is possible; it is true that even there many egos are only slightly and dreamily conscious of their surroundings, but in so far as they see, they see truly, for thought no longer assumes the same deceptive forms which it took upon itself lower down.

THE ACTION OF THOUGHT.

The exact condition of mind of the human inhabitants of these various sub-planes will naturally be much more fully dealt with under its own appropriate heading; but a comprehension of the manner in which thought acts in the rûpa and arûpa levels respectively is so necessary to an accurate understanding of these great divisions that it will perhaps be worth while to recount in detail some of the experiments made by our explorers in the endeavour to throw light upon this subject.

At an early period of the investigation it became evident that on the devachanic as on the astral plane there was present an elemental essence quite distinct from the mere matter of the plane, and that it was, if possible, even more instantaneously sensitive to the action of thought here than it had been in that lower world. But here in Devachan *all* was thought-substance, and therefore not only the elemental essence, but the very matter of the plane was directly affected by the action of the mind; and hence it became necessary to make an attempt to discriminate between these two effects.

After various less conclusive experiments a method was adopted which gave a fairly clear idea of the different results produced, one investigator remaining on the lowest subdivision to send out the thought-forms, while others rose to the next higher level, so as to be able to observe what took place from above, and thus avoid many possibilities of confusion. Under these circumstances the experiment was tried of sending an affectionate and helpful thought to an absent friend. The result was very remarkable; a sort of vibrating shell, formed in the matter of the plane, issued in all directions round the operator, corresponding exactly to the circle which spreads out in still water from the spot where a stone has been thrown into it, except that this was a sphere of vibration extending itself in three (or perhaps four) dimensions instead of merely over a flat surface. These vibrations, like those on the physical plane, though very much more gradually, lost in intensity as they passed further away from their source, till at last at an enormous distance they seemed to be exhausted, or at least became so faint as to be imperceptible. Thus every one on the devachanic plane is a centre of radiant thought, and yet all the rays thrown out cross in all directions without interfering with one another in the slightest degree, just as rays of light do down here. This expanding sphere of vibrations was many coloured and opalescent, but its colours also grew gradually fainter and fainter as it spread away.

The effect on the elemental essence of the plane was, however, entirely different. In this the thought immediately called into existence a distinct form resembling the human, of one colour only, though exhibiting many shades of that colour. This form flashed across the ocean with the speed of thought to the friend to whom the good wish had been directed, and there took to itself elemental essence of the astral plane, and thus became an ordinary artificial elemental of that plane, waiting, as explained in Manual No. V., for an opportunity to pour out upon him its store of helpful influence. In taking on that astral form the devachanic elemental lost much of its brilliancy, though its glowing rose-colour was still plainly visible inside the shell of lower matter which it had assumed, showing that just as the original thought ensouled the elemental essence of its own plane, so that same thought, plus its form as a devachanic elemental, acted as soul to the astral elemental—thus following closely the method in which Âtmâ itself takes on sheath after sheath in its descent through the various planes and sub-planes of matter.

Further experiments along similar lines revealed the fact that the colour of the elemental sent forth varied with the character of the thought. As above stated, the thought of strong affection produced a creature of glowing rose-colour; an intense wish of healing, projected towards a sick friend, called into existence a most lovely silvery-white elemental; while an earnest mental effort to steady and strengthen the mind of a depressed and despairing person resulted in the production of a beautiful flashing golden-yellow messenger.

In all these cases it will be perceived that, besides the effect of radiating colours and vibrations produced in the matter of the plane, a definite force in the shape of an elemental was sent forth towards the person to whom the thought was directed; and this invariably happened, with one notable exception. One of the operators, while on the lower division of the plane, directed a thought of intense love and devotion towards the Adept who is his spiritual teacher, and it was at once noticed by the observers above that the result was in some sense a reversal of what had happened in the previous cases.

It should be premised that a pupil of any one of the great Adepts is always connected with his Master by a constant current of thought and influence, which expresses itself on the devachanic plane as a great ray or stream of dazzling light of all colours—violet and gold and blue; and it might perhaps have been expected that the pupil's earnest, loving thought would send a special vibration along this line. Instead of this, however, the result was a sudden intensification of the colours of this bar of light, and a very distinct flow of magnetic influence *towards the pupil;* so that it is evident that when a student turns his thought to the Master, what he really does is to vivify his connection with that Master, and thus to open a way for an additional out-pouring of strength and help to himself from higher planes. It would seem that the Adept is, as it were, so highly charged with the influences which sustain and strengthen, that any thought which brings into increased activity a channel of communication with him sends no current towards him, as it ordinarily would, but simply gives a wider opening through which the great ocean of his love finds vent.

On the arûpa levels the difference in the effect of thought is very marked, especially as regards the elemental essence. The disturbance set up in the mere matter of the plane is similar, though greatly intensified in this much more refined form of matter; but in the essence no form at all is now created, and the method of action is entirely changed. In all the experiments on lower planes it was found that the elemental produced hovered about the person thought of, and awaited a favourable opportunity of expending his energy either upon his mind-body, his astral, or even his physical body; here the result is a kind of lightning-flash of the essence from the causal body of the thinker direct to the causal body of the object of his thought; so that while the thought on those lower divisions is always directed to the mere personality, here you influence the reincarnating ego, the real man himself, and if your message has any reference to the personality it will reach it only from above, through the instrumentality of the Kârana Sharîra.

THOUGHT-FORMS.

Naturally the thoughts to be seen on this plane are not all definitely directed at some other person; many are simply thrown off to float vaguely about, and the diversity of form and colour shown among these is practically infinite, so that the study of them is a science in itself, and a very fascinating one. Anything like a detailed description even of the main classes among them would occupy far more space than we have to spare; but an idea of the principles upon. Which such classes might be formed may be gained from the following extract from a most illuminative paper on the subject written by Mrs. Besant in *Lucifer* for September, 1896. She there enunciates the three great principles underlying the production of thought-forms—that (*a*) the quality of a thought determines its colour, (*b*) the nature of a thought determines its form, (*c*) the definiteness of a thought determines the clearness of its outline. Giving instances of the way in which the colour is affected, she continues:

"If the astral and mental bodies are vibrating under the influence of devotion, the aura will be suffused with blue, more or less intense, beautiful and pure according to the depth, elevation and purity of the feeling. In a church such thought-forms may be seen rising, for the most part not very definitely outlined, but rolling masses of blue clouds. Too often the colour is dulled by the intermixture of selfish feelings, when the blue is mixed with browns and thus loses its pure brilliancy. But the devotional thought of an unselfish heart is very lovely in colour, like the deep blue of a summer sky. Through such clouds of blue will often shine out golden stars of great brilliancy, starting upwards like a shower of sparks.

"Anger gives rise to red, of all shades from brick-red to brilliant scarlet; brutal anger will show as flashes of lurid dull red from dark brown clouds, while the anger of 'noble indignation' is a vivid scarlet, by no means unbeautiful to look at though it gives an unpleasant thrill.

"Affection sends out clouds of rosy hue, varying from dull crimson, where the love is animal in its nature, rose-red mingled with brown when selfish, or with dull green when jealous, to the most exquisite shades of delicate rose like the early flushes of the dawning, as the love becomes purified from all selfish elements, and flows out in wider and wider circles of generous impersonal tenderness and compassion to all who are in need.

"Intellect produces yellow thought-forms, the pure reason directed to spiritual ends giving rise to a very delicate, beautiful yellow, while used for more selfish ends or mingled with ambition it yields deeper shades of orange, clear and intense" *(Lucifer,* vol. xix. p. 71).

It must of course be borne in mind that astral as well as mental thought-forms are described in the above quotation, some of the feelings mentioned needing matter of the lower plane as well as of the higher before they can find expression. Some examples are then given of the beautiful flower-like and shell-like forms sometimes taken by our nobler thoughts; and especial reference is made to the not infrequent case in which the thought, taking human form, is liable to be confounded with an apparition:

"A thought-form may assume the shape of its projector; if a person wills strongly to be present at a particular place, to visit a particular person, and be seen, such a thought-form may take his own shape, and a clairvoyant present at the desired spot would see what he would probably mistake for his friend in the astral body. Such a thought-form might convey a message, if that formed part of its content, setting up in the astral body of the person reached vibrations like its own, and these being passed on by that astral body to the brain, where they would be translated into a thought or a sentence. Such a thought-form, again, might convey to its projector, by the magnetic relation between them, vibrations impressed on itself" (p. 73).

The whole of the article from which these extracts are taken should be very carefully studied by those who wish to grasp this very complex branch of our subject, for, with the aid of the beautifully-executed coloured illustrations which accompany it, it enables those who cannot yet see for themselves to approach much more nearly to a realization of what thought-forms actually are than anything previously written.

THE SUB-PLANES.

If it be asked what is the real difference between the matter of the various sub-planes of Devachan, it is not easy to answer in other than very general terms, for the unfortunate scribe bankrupts himself of adjectives in an unsuccessful endeavour to describe the lowest plane, and then has nothing left to say about the others. What, indeed, can be said, except that ever as we ascend the material becomes finer, the harmonies fuller, the light more living and transparent? There are more over-tones in the sound, more delicate intershades in the colours as we rise, more and more new colours appear—hues entirely unknown to the physical sight; and it has been poetically yet truly said that the light of the lower plane is darkness on the one above it. Perhaps this idea is simpler if we start in thought from the top instead of the bottom, and try to realize that on that highest sub-plane we shall find its appropriate matter ensouled and vivified by an energy which still flows down like light from above—from a plane which lies away beyond Devachan altogether. Then if we descend to the second subdivision we shall find that the matter of our first sub-plane has become the energy of this—or, to put the thing more accurately, that the original energy, plus the garment of matter of the first sub-plane with which it has endued itself, is the energy of this second sub-plane. In the same way, in the third division we shall find that the original energy has twice veiled itself in the matter of these first and second sub-planes through which it has passed; so that by the time we get to our seventh subdivision we shall have our original energy six times enclosed or veiled, and therefore by so much the weaker and less active. This process is exactly analogous to the veiling of Âtmâ in its descent as monadic essence in order to energize the matter of the planes of the cosmos, and as it is one which frequently takes place in nature, it will save the student much trouble if he will try to familiarize himself with the idea.

THE ÂKÂSHIC RECORDS.

In speaking of the general characteristics of the plane we must not omit to mention the âkâshic records, which form what may be called the memory of nature, the only really reliable history of the world. Whether what we have on this plane is the absolute record itself or merely a devachanic reflection of something higher still, it is at any rate clear, accurate, and continuous, differing therein from the disconnected and spasmodic manifestation which is all that represents it in the astral world. It is, therefore, only when a clairvoyant possesses the vision of this devachanic plane that his pictures of the past can be relied upon; and even then, unless he has the power of passing in full consciousness from that plane to the physical we have to allow for the possibility of errors in bringing back the recollection of what he has seen.

But the student who has succeeded in developing the powers latent within himself so far as to enable him to use the devachanic sense while still in the physical body, has before him a field of historical research of most entrancing interest. Not only can he review at his leisure all history with which we are acquainted, correcting as he examines it the many errors and misconceptions which have crept into the accounts handed down to us; he can also range at will over the whole story of the world from its very beginning, watching the slow development of intellect in man, the descent of the Lords of the Flame, and the growth of the mighty civilizations which they founded.

Nor is his study confined to the progress of humanity alone; he has before him, as in a museum, all the strange animal and vegetable forms which occupied the stage in days when the world was young; he can follow all the wonderful geological changes which have taken place, and watch the course of the great cataclysms which have altered the whole face of the earth again and again.

Many and varied are the possibilities opened up. by access to the âkâshic records—so many and so varied indeed that even if this were the only advantage of the devachanic plane it would still transcend in interest all the lower worlds; but when to this we add the remarkable increase in the opportunities for the acquisition of knowledge given by its new and wider faculty—the privilege of direct untram-melled intercourse not only with the great Deva kingdom, but with the very Masters of Wisdom themselves—the rest and relief from the weary strain of physical life that is brought by the enjoyment of its deep unchanging bliss, and above all the enormously enhanced capability of the developed student for the service of his fellow-men—then we shall begin to have some faint conception of what a pupil gains when he wins the right to enter at will and in perfect consciousness upon his heritage in the bright realm of Sukhâvatî.

INHABITANTS.

In our endeavour to describe the inhabitants of Devachan it will perhaps be well for us to divide them into the same three great classes chosen in the manual on the astral plane—the human, the non-human, and the artificial—though the subdivisions will naturally be less numerous in this case than in that, since the products of man's evil passions, which bulked so largely in Kâmaloka, can find no place here.

I. HUMAN.

Exactly as was the case when dealing with the lower world, it will be desirable to subdivide the human inhabitants of the devachanic plane into two classes—those who are still attached to a physical body, and those who are not—the living and the dead, as they are commonly but most erroneously called. Very little experience of these higher planes is needed to alter fundamentally the student's conception of the change which takes place at death; he realizes immediately on the opening of his consciousness even in the astral, and still more in the devachanic world, that the fulness of true life is something which can never be known down here, and that when we leave this physical earth we are passing *into* that true life, not out of it. We have not at present in the English language any convenient and at the same time accurate words to express these conditions; perhaps to call them respectively embodied and disembodied will be, on the whole, the least misleading of the various possible phrases. Let us therefore proceed to consider those inhabitants of Devachan who come under the head of

THE EMBODIED.

Those human beings who, while still attached to a physical body, are found moving in full consciousness and activity upon this plane are invariably either initiates or Adepts, for until a pupil has been taught by his Master how to form the Mâyâvirûpa he will be unable to move with freedom upon even the rûpa levels of Devachan. To function consciously during physical life upon the arûpa levels denotes still greater advancement, for it means the unification of the Manas, so that the man down here is no longer a mere personality, more or less influenced by the individuality above, but is himself that individuality—trammelled and confined by a body, certainly, but nevertheless having within him the power and knowledge of a highly developed ego.

Very magnificent objects are these Adepts and initiates to the vision which has learnt to see them—splendid globes of light and colour, driving away all evil influence wherever they go, and shedding around them a feeling of restfulness and happiness of which even those who do not see them are often conscious. It is in this celestial world that much of their most important work is done—more especially upon its higher levels, where the individuality can be acted upon directly. It is from this plane that they shower the grandest spiritual influences upon the world of thought; from it also they impel great and beneficent movements of all kinds. Here much of the spiritual force poured out by the glorious self-sacrifice of the Nirmânâkayas is distributed; here also direct teaching is given to those pupils who are sufficiently advanced to receive it in this way, since it can be imparted far more readily and completely than on the astral plane. In addition to all these activities they have a great field of work in connection with devachanees, but this will be more fitly explained under a later heading.

It is a pleasure to find that a class of inhabitants which obtruded itself painfully on our notice on the astral plane is entirely absent here. In a world whose characteristics are unselfishness and spirituality the black magician and his pupils can obviously find no place, since selfishness is of the essence of all the proceedings of the darker school. Not but that in many of them the intellect is very highly developed, and consequently the matter of the mind-body extremely active and sensitive along certain lines; but in every case those lines are connected with personal desire of some sort, and they can therefore find expression only through Kâma-Manas—that is, the part of the mind-body which has become almost inextricably entangled with Kama. As a necessary consequence of this limitation it follows that their activities are confined to the astral and physical planes, and thus is justified the grand old description of the heaven-world as the place "where the wicked cease from troubling, and the weary are at rest."

IN SLEEP OR TRANCE.

In thinking of the living inhabitants of Devachan, the question naturally suggests itself whether either ordinary people during sleep, or psychically developed persons in a trance condition, can ever penetrate to this plane. In both cases the answer must be that the occurrence is possible, though extremely rare. Purity of life and purpose would be an absolute pre-requisite, and even when the plane was reached there would be nothing that could be called real consciousness, but simply a capacity for receiving certain impressions.

As exemplifying the possibility of entering the devachanic state during sleep, an incident may be mentioned which occurred in connection with the experiments made by the London Lodge of the Theosophical Society on dream consciousness, an account of some of which was given in their Transaction on *Dreams*. It may be remembered by those who have read that Transaction that a thought-picture of a lovely tropical landscape was presented to the minds of various classes of sleepers, with a view of testing the extent to which it was afterwards recollected on awaking. One case which was not referred to in the account previously published, as it had no special connection with the phenomena of dreams, will serve as a useful illustration here.

It was that of a person of pure mind and considerable though untrained psychic capacity; and the effect of the presentation of the thought-picture to her mind was of a somewhat startling character. So intense was the feeling of reverent joy, so lofty and so spiritual were the thoughts evoked by the contemplation of this glorious scene, that the consciousness of the sleeper passed entirely into the mind-body—or to put the same idea into other words, rose on to the devachanic plane. It must not, however, he supposed from this that she became cognizant of her surroundings upon that plane, or of its real conditions; she was simply in the state of the ordinary devachanee after death, floating in the sea of light and colour indeed, but entirely absorbed in her own thought, and conscious of nothing beyond it—resting in ecstatic contemplation of the landscape and of all that it had suggested to her—yet contemplating it, be it understood, with the keener insight, the more perfect appreciation, and the enhanced vigour of thought peculiar to the devachanic plane, and enjoying all the while the intensity of bliss which has so often been spoken of before. The sleeper remained in that condition for several hours, though apparently entirely unconscious of the passage of time, and at last awoke with a sense of deep peace and inward joy for which, since she had brought back no recollection of what had happened, she was quite unable to account. There is no doubt, however, that such an experience as this, whether remembered in the physical body or not, would act as a distinct impulse to the spiritual evolution of the ego concerned.

Though in the absence of a sufficient number of experiments one hesitates to speak too positively, it seems almost certain that such a result as this just described would be possible only in the case of a person having already some amount of psychic development; and the same condition is even more definitely necessary in order that a mesmerized subject should touch the devachanic plane in trance. So decidedly is this the case, that probably not one in a thousand among ordinary clairvoyants ever reaches it at all; but on the rare occasions when it is so attained the clairvoyant, as before remarked, must be not only of exceptional development, but of perfect purity of life and purpose: and even when all these unusual characteristics are present there still remains the difficulty which an untrained psychic always finds in translating a vision accurately from the higher plane to the lower. All these considerations, of course, only emphasize what has been so often insisted upon before—the necessity of the careful training of all psychics under a qualified instructor before it is possible to attach much weight to their reports of what they see.

THE DISEMBODIED.

Before considering in detail the condition of the disembodied entities on the various sub-planes of Devachan, we must have very clearly in our minds the broad distinction between the rûpa and arûpa levels, of which mention has already been made. On the former the man lives entirely in the world of his own thoughts, still fully identifying himself with his personality in the life which he has recently quitted; on the latter he is simply the reincarnating ego, who (if he has developed sufficient consciousness on that level to know anything clearly at all) understands, at least to some extent, the evolution upon which he is engaged, and the work that he has to do. It should be remembered that every man passes through both these stages between death and birth, though the undeveloped majority have so-little consciousness in either of them as yet that they might more truly he said to dream through them. Nevertheless, whether consciously or unconsciously, every human being must touch his own ego on the arûpa level of Devachan before reincarnation can take place: and as his evolution proceeds this touch becomes more and more definite and real to him. Not only is he more conscious here as he progresses, but the period he passes in this world of reality becomes longer; for the fact is that his consciousness is slowly but steadily rising through the different planes of the system.

Primitive man, for example, would have comparatively little consciousness on any plane but the physical during life and the lower astral after death; and indeed the same may be said of the quite undeveloped man even in our own day. A person a little more advanced would perhaps begin to have a short devachanic period (on the rûpa levels, of course), but would still spend by far the greater part of his time, between incarnations, on the astral plane. As he progressed the astral life would grow shorter and the devachanic life longer, until when he became an intellectual and spiritually-minded person he would pass through Kâmaloka with hardly any delay at all, and would enjoy a long and happy sojourn on the higher of the rûpa levels. By this time, however, the consciousness in the true ego on the arûpa levels would have been awakened to a very considerable extent, and thus his conscious life

16

in Devachan would divide itself into two parts—the later and shorter portion being spent on the higher sub-planes in the causal body.

The process previously described would then repeat itself, the life on the rûpa levels gradually shortening, while the higher life became steadily longer and fuller, till at last the time came when the consciousness was unified—when the higher and lower Manas were indissolubly united, and the man was no longer capable of wrapping himself up in his own cloud of thought, and mistaking that for the great heaven-world around him—when he realized the true possibilities of his life, and so for the first time truly began to live. But by the time that he attains these heights he will already be an initiate, and will have taken his future progress definitely into his own hands.

IS THE DEVACHANIC LIFE AN ILLUSION.

It has frequently been urged, as an objection to the Theosophical teaching on the subject of the hereafter, that the life of the ordinary person in Devachan is nothing but a dream and an illusion—that when he imagines himself happy amidst his family and friends, or carrying out his plans with such fulness of joy and success, he is really only the victim of a cruel delusion: and this is sometimes unfavourably contrasted with what is called the solid objectivity of the heaven promised by Christianity. The reply to such an objection is twofold: first, that when we are studying the problems of the future life we are not concerned to know which of two hypotheses put before us would be the pleasanter (that being, after all, a matter of opinion), but rather which of them is the true one; and secondly, that when we enquire more fully into the facts of the case we shall see that those who maintain the illusion theory are looking at the matter from quite a wrong point of view.

As to the first point, the actual state of the facts is quite easily discoverable by those who have developed the power to pass consciously on to the devachanic plane during life; and when so investigated it is found to agree perfectly with the teaching given to us by the Masters of Wisdom through our great founder and teacher Madame Blavatsky. This, of course, disposes of the "solid objectivity" theory mentioned above. As to the second point, if the contention be that on the lower levels of Devachan truth in its fulness is not yet known to man, and that consequently illusion still exists there, we must frankly admit that that is so. But that is not what is usually meant by those who bring forward this objection; they are generally oppressed by a feeling that the devachanic life will be more illusory and useless than the physical—an idea which further consideration will, I think, show to be in-accurate.

Let it be clearly grasped first of all that such illusion as there is inheres in the personality, and that when that is for the time dissipated no illusion remains. (Of course I am using the word illusion in its ordinary everyday meaning—not in that metaphysical sense in which all is illusion until the absolute is attained.) It will be seen, as our account of the plane progresses, that this illusion differs very much on different levels, and that it steadily diminishes as the soul advances. Indeed, we may say that just as it is only the child down here who constantly "makes believe," so it is only the child-soul who surrounds himself again and again with an illusory world created by his own thoughts.

In point of fact, the Devachan of each person is exactly suited to him; as *he* becomes more real, *it* becomes more real also. And we ought in fairness to bear in mind, before inveighing against the unreality of Devachan, that we are, after all, at the present moment living a life which is still more unreal. Is it contended that on that plane we make our own surroundings, and that they have therefore no objective existence? But surely that argument cuts both ways: for even down here the world of which a person is sensible is never the *whole* of the outer world, but only so much of it as his senses, his intellect, his education, enable him to take in. It is obvious that during life the average person's conception of everything around him is really quite a wrong one—empty, imperfect, inaccurate in a dozen ways; for what does he know of the great forces—etheric, astral, devachanic—which lie behind everything he sees, and in fact form by far the most important part of it? What does he know, as a rule, even of the more recondite physical facts which surround him and meet him at every step that he takes? The truth is that here, as in Devachan, he lives in a world which is very largely of his own creation. He does not realize it, of course, either there or here, but that is only because of his ignorance—because he knows no better.

It may be thought that there is a difference in the case of our friends—that here we have them really with us, whereas in Devachan what we have is only an image of them which we ourselves make. This latter statement is true only of the lowest planes, and if the friend is an entirely undeveloped person; but, once more, is not the case exactly the same down here? Here also we see our friend only partly—we know only the part of him which is congenial to us, and the other sides of his character are practically nonexistent for us. If we were for the first time, and with the direct and perfect vision of the devachanic plane, to see the *whole* of our friend, the probability is that he would be quite unrecognizable: certainly he would not be at all the dear one whom we had known.

Not only is it true that as a man becomes more real himself his Devachan becomes more real; it is also a fact that, as the man evolves, the image of him in his friend's Devachan becomes more real too. This was very well illustrated by a simple case which recently came under the notice of our investigators. It was that of a mother who had died perhaps twenty years ago, leaving behind her two boys to whom she was deeply attached. Naturally they were the most prominent figures in her Devachan, and quite naturally, too, she thought of them as she had left them, as boys of fifteen or sixteen years of age. The love which she thus ceaselessly poured out upon these images in Devachan was really acting as a beneficent force showered down upon the grown-up men in this physical world, but it did not affect them both to the same extent—not that her love was stronger for one than the other, but because there was a great difference between the images themselves. Not a difference, be it understood, that the mother could see; to her both appeared equally with her and equally all that she could possibly desire: yet to the eyes of the investigators it was very evident that one of these images was a mere thought-form of the mother's, without anything that could be called a reality at the back of it, while the other was distinctly much more than a mere image, for it was instinct with living force. On tracing this very interesting phenomenon to its source, it was found that in the first case the son had grown up into an ordinary man of business—not specially evil in any way, but by no means spiritually-minded—while the second had become a man of high unselfish aspiration, and of considerable refinement and culture. His life had been such as to develope a much greater amount of consciousness in the ego than his brother's, and consequently his higher self was able to energize the image of himself as a boy which his mother had formed in her Devachan—to put something of himself into it, as it were.

A large number of similar instances were revealed by further research, and it was eventually clearly established that the more highly a man is developed along spiritual lines, the more truly is his image in his friend's Devachan informed by a ray from his higher ego, even though the personality down here in incarnation may often be entirely ignorant of its action. Thus as the man rises his image becomes more really himself, until in the case of an Adept that image is fully and consciously entered and used as a means of raising and instructing the pupil who has formed it. Of this more will be said later; but meantime it is abundantly evident that, as man evolves, the illusions which clung round his spiritual childhood drop away, and he draws ever nearer and nearer to the reality which lies behind them.

In this manner, and in this manner only, is communication possible between those who still live on earth and those who have passed into this celestial realm. A man's higher self may be informing his image in a friend's Devachan, and yet the living man here on earth may know nothing of it, and therefore remain quite unable to communicate with his departed friend; but if the living man has evolved his consciousness to the point of unification, and can therefore use the powers of the ego while still in the physical body, he can enter at will and in full consciousness into that image of his, and can speak once more face to face with his friend, as of yore: so that in such a case the "devachanic dream" is no longer an illusion, but a living reality.

Is it said that on the devachanic plane a man takes his thoughts for real things? He is quite right; they *are* real things, and on this, the thought-plane, nothing but thought *can* be real. There we recognize that great fact—here we do not; on which plane, then, is the delusion greater? Those thoughts of the devachanee are indeed realities, and are capable of producing the most striking results upon living men— results which can never be otherwise than beneficial, because upon that high plane there can be none but loving thought.

Another point worth bearing in mind is that this system upon which nature has arranged the life after death is the only imaginable one which could fulfil its object of making every one happy to the fullest extent of his capacity for happiness. If the joy of heaven were of one particular type only, as it is according to the orthodox Christian theory, there must always he some who would weary of it, some who would be incapable of participating in it, either from want of taste in that particular direction, or from lack of the necessary education—to say nothing of that other obvious fact, that if this condition of affairs were eternal the grossest injustice must be perpetrated by giving practically the same reward to all who enter, no matter what their respective deserts might be.

Again, what other arrangement with regard to relatives and friends could possibly be equally satisfactory? If the departed were able to follow the fluctuating fortunes of their friends on earth, happiness would be impossible for them; if, without knowing what was happening to them, they had to wait until the death of those friends before meeting them, there would he a painful period of suspense, often extending over many years, while the friend would in many cases arrive so much changed as to be no longer sympathetic.

On the system so wisely provided for us by nature every one of these difficulties is avoided; a man decides for himself both the length and the character of his Devachan by the causes which he himself generates during his earth-life; therefore he cannot but have exactly the amount which he has deserved, and exactly that quality of joy which is best suited to his idiosyncrasies. Those whom he loves most he has ever with him, and always at their noblest and best; while no shadow of discord or change can ever come between them, since he receives from them all the time exactly what he wishes. In point of fact, as we might have expected, the arrangement really made by nature is infinitely superior to anything which the imagination of man has been able to offer us in its place.

THE QUALITIES NECESSARY FOR DEVACHANIC LIFE.

The greater reality of the devachanic life as compared with that on earth is again evidenced when we consider what conditions are requisite for the attainment of this higher state of existence. For the very qualities which a man must develope during life, if he is to have any Devachan after death, are just those which all the best and noblest of our race have agreed in considering as really and permanently desirable. In order that an aspiration or a thought-force should result in existence on that plane, its dominant characteristic must be unselfishness.

Affection for family or friends takes many a man into Devachan, and so also does religious devotion; yet it would be a mistake to suppose that *all* affection or all devotion must therefore necessarily find its *post-mortem* expression there, for of each of these qualities there are obviously two varieties, the selfish and the unselfish—though it might perhaps reasonably be argued that it is only the latter kind in each case which is really worthy of the name.

There is the love which pours itself out upon its object, seeking for nothing in return—never even thinking of itself, but only of what it can do for the loved one and such a feeling as this generates a spiritual force which cannot work itself out except upon the devachanic plane. But there is also another emotion which is sometimes called love—an exacting, selfish kind of passion which desires mainly to *be* loved—which is thinking all the time of what it receives rather than of what it gives, and is quite likely to degenerate into the horrible vice of jealousy upon (or even without) the smallest provocation. Such affection as this has in it no seed of devachanic development; the forces which it sets in motion will never rise above the astral plane.

The same is true of the feeling of a certain very large class of religious devotees, whose one thought is, not the glory of their deity, but how they may save their own miserable souls—a position which forcibly suggests that they have not yet developed anything that really deserves the name of a soul at all.

On the other hand there is the real religious devotion, which thinks never of self, but only of love and gratitude towards the deity or leader, and is filled with ardent desire to do something for him or in his name; and such a feeling often leads to prolonged Devachan of a comparatively exalted type.

This would of course be the case whoever the deity or leader might be, and followers of Buddha, Krishna, Ormuzd, Allah and Christ would all equally attain their need of devachanic bliss—its length and quality depending upon the intensity and purity of the feeling, and not in the least upon its object, though this latter consideration would undoubtedly affect the possibility of receiving instruction during that higher life.

Most human devotion, however, like most human love, is neither wholly pure nor wholly selfish. That love must be low indeed into which no unselfish thought or impulse has entered; and on the other hand an affection which is usually and chiefly quite pure and noble may yet sometimes be clouded by a spasm of jealous feeling or a passing thought of self. In both these cases, as in all, Karma discriminates unerringly; and just as the momentary flash of nobler feeling in the less developed heart will receive its devachanic meed even though there be nought else in the life to raise the soul above the astral plane, so the baser thought which erstwhile dimmed the holy radiance of a real love will reap its due reward in Kâmaloka, interfering not at all with the magnificent celestial life which flows infallibly from years of deep affection here below.

How a Man first gains Devachan.

It will be seen, therefore, that many undeveloped and backward egos never consciously attain the devachanic state at all, whilst a still larger number obtain only a comparatively slight touch of some of its lower planes. Every ego must of course withdraw into its true self upon the arûpa levels before reincarnation; but it does not at all follow that in that condition it will experience anything that we should call consciousness. This subject will be dealt with more fully when we come to treat of the arûpa planes; it seems better to begin with the lowest of the rûpa levels, and work steadily upwards, so we may for the moment leave on one side that portion of humanity whose conscious existence after death is practically confined to the astral plane, and proceed to consider the case of an entity who has just risen out of that position—who for the first time has a slight and fleeting consciousness in the lowest subdivision of Devachan.

There are evidently various methods by which this important step in the early development of the ego may be brought about, but it will be sufficient for our present purpose if we take as an illustration of one of them a somewhat pathetic little story from real life which came under the observation of our students when they were investigating this question. In this case the agent of the great evolutionary forces was a poor seamstress, living in one of the dreariest and most squalid of our terrible London slums—a foetid court in the East End into which light and air could scarcely struggle.

Naturally she was not highly educated, for her life had been one long round of the hardest work under the least favourable of conditions; but nevertheless she was a good-hearted, benevolent creature, overflowing with love and kindness towards all with whom she came into contact. Her rooms were as poor, perhaps, as any in the court, but at least they were cleaner and neater than the others. She had no money to give when sickness brought need even more dire than usual to some of her neighbours, yet on such an occasion she was always at hand as often as she could snatch a few moments from her work, offering with ready sympathy such service as was within her power.

Indeed, she was quite a providence to the rough, ignorant factory girls about her, and they gradually came to look upon her as a kind of angel of help and mercy, always at hand in time of trouble or illness. Often after toiling all day with scarcely a moment's intermission she sat up half the night, taking her turn at nursing some of the many sufferers who are always to be found in surroundings so fatal to health and happiness as those of a London slum; and in many cases the gratitude and affection which her unremitting kindness aroused in them were absolutely the only higher feelings that they had during the whole of their rough and sordid lives.

21

The conditions of existence in that court being such as they were, there is little wonder that some of her patients died, and then it became clear that she had done for them much more than she knew; she had given them not only a little kindly assistance in their temporal trouble, but a very important impulse on the course of spiritual evolution. For these were undeveloped egos—pitris of a very backward class—who had never yet in any of their births set in motion the spiritual forces which alone could give them conscious existence on the devachanic plane; but now for the first time not only had an ideal towards which they could strive been put before them, but also really unselfish love had been evoked in them by her action, and the very fact of having so strong a feeling as this had raised them and given them more individuality, and so after their stay in Kâmaloka was ended they gained their first experience of the lowest subdivision of Devachan. A short experience, probably, and of by no means an advanced type, but still of far greater importance than appears at first sight; for when once the great spiritual energy of unselfishness has been awakened the very working-out of its results in Devachan gives it the tendency to repeat itself, and small in amount though this first outpouring may be, it yet builds into the ego a faint tinge of a quality which will certainly express itself again in the next life.

So the gentle benevolence of a poor seamstress has given to several less developed souls their introduction to a conscious spiritual life which incarnation after incarnation will grow steadily stronger, and react more and more upon the earth-lives of the future. This little incident perhaps suggests an explanation of the fact that in the various religions so much importance is attached to the personal element in charity—the direct association between donor and recipient.

SEVENTH SUB-PLANE.

This lowest subdivision of Devachan, to which the action of our poor seamstress raised the objects of her kindly care, has for its principal characteristic that of affection for family or friends—unselfish, of course, but usually somewhat narrow. Here, however, we must guard ourselves against the possibility of misconception. When it is said that family affection takes a man to the seventh devachanic sub-plane, and religious devotion to the sixth, people sometimes very naturally imagine that a person having both these characteristics strongly developed in him would divide his devachanic period between these two subdivisions, first spending a long period of happiness in the midst of his family, and then passing upward to the next level, there to exhaust the spiritual forces engendered by his devotional aspirations.

This, however, is not what happens, for in such a case as we have supposed the man would awaken to consciousness in the sixth sub-division, where he would find himself engaged, together with those whom he had loved so much, in the highest form of devotion which he was able to realize. And when we think of it this is reasonable enough, for the man who is capable of religious devotion as well as mere family affection is naturally likely to be endowed with a higher and broader development of the latter virtue than one whose mind is susceptible to influence in one direction only. The same rule holds good all the way up; the higher plane may always include the qualities of the lower as well as those peculiar to itself, and when it does so its inhabitants almost invariably have these qualities in fuller measure than the souls on a lower plane.

When it is said that family affection is the characteristic of the seventh sub-plane, it must not therefore be supposed for a moment that love is confined to this plane, but rather that the man who will find himself here after death is one in whose character this affection was the highest quality—the only one, in fact, which entitled him to Devachan at all. But love of a far nobler and grander type than anything to be seen on this level may of course be found upon the higher sub-planes.

One of the first entities encountered by the investigators upon this sub-plane forms a very fair typical example of its inhabitants. The man during life had been a small grocer—not a person of intellectual development or of any particular religious feeling, but simply the ordinary honest and respectable small tradesman. No doubt he had gone to church regularly every Sunday, because it was the customary and proper thing to do; but religion had been to him a sort of dim cloud which he did not really understand, which had no connection with the business of everyday life, and was never taken into account in deciding its problems. He had therefore none of the depth of devotion which might have lifted him to the next sub-plane; but he had for his wife and family a warm affection in which there was a large element of unselfishness. They were constantly in his mind, and it was for them far more than for himself that he worked from morning to night in his tiny little shop; and so when, after a period of existence in Kâmaloka, he had at last shaken himself free from the decaying astral body, he found himself upon this lowest subdivision of Devachan with all his loved ones gathered round him.

He was no more an intellectual or highly spiritual man than he had been on earth, for death brings with it no sudden development of that kind; the surroundings in which he found himself with his family were not of a very refined type, for they represented only his own highest ideals of non-physical enjoyment during life; but nevertheless he was as intensely happy as he was capable of being, and since he was all the time thinking of his family rather than of himself he was undoubtedly developing unselfish characteristics, which would be built into the ego, and so would reappear in his next life on earth.

Another typical case was that of a man who had died while his only daughter was still young; here in Devachan he had her always with him and always at her best, and he was continually occupying himself in weaving all sorts of beautiful pictures of her future. Yet another was that of a young girl who was always absorbed in contemplating the manifold perfections of her father, and planning little surprises and fresh pleasures for him. Another was a Greek woman who was spending a marvellously happy time with her three children—one of them a beautiful boy, whom she delighted in imagining as the victor in the Olympic games.

A striking characteristic of this sub-plane for the last few centuries has been the very large number of Romans, Carthaginians and English-men to be found there—this being due to the fact that among men of these nations the principal unselfish activity found its outlet through family affection; while comparatively few Hindus and Buddhists are here, since in their case real religious feeling usually enters more immediately into their daily lives, and consequently takes them to a higher level.

There was, of course, an almost infinite variety among the cases observed, their different degrees of advancement being distinguishable by varying degrees of luminosity, while differences of colour indicated respectively the qualities which the persons in question had developed. Some were lovers who had died in the full strength of their affection, and so were always occupied with the one person they loved to the entire exclusion of all others; others there were who had been almost savages, one example being a Malay, a low third-class pitri, who obtained a slight experience of Devachan in connection with a daughter whom he had loved.

In all these cases it was the touch of unselfish affection which gave them their Devachan; indeed, apart from that, there was nothing in the activity of their personal lives which could have expressed itself on that plane. In most instances observed on this level the images of the loved ones have in them but the faintest glimmer of real vitality, owing to the fact that naturally in the vast majority of cases their individualities have not been developed into activity on this plane. Of course wherever such development has taken place the image would be vivified by a ray of the higher self of the person whom it represented, and much benefit might he derived by the devachanee from his intercourse with it.

Before passing on to consider the higher levels it would be well perhaps to refer to the way in which consciousness is recovered upon entering the devachanic plane. On the final separation of the mind-body from the astral a period of blank unconsciousness supervenes—varying in length between very wide limits—analogous to that which usually follows physical death. The awakening from this into active devachanic consciousness closely resembles what often occurs in waking from a night's sleep. Just as on first awakening in the morning one sometimes passes through a period of intensely delightful repose during which one is conscious of the sense of enjoyment, though the mind is as yet inactive and the body hardly under control, so the entity awakening on the devachanic plane first passes through a more or less prolonged period of intense and gradually increasing bliss before his full activity of consciousness on that plane is reached. When first this sense of wondrous joy dawns on him it fills the entire field of his consciousness, but gradually as he awakens he finds himself surrounded by a world of his own creation presenting the features appropriate to the sub-plane to which he has been drawn.

Sixth Sub-Plane.

The dominant characteristic of this subdivision appears to be anthropomorphic religious devotion. The distinction between such devotion and the religious feeling which finds its expression on the second sub-plane of the astral lies in the fact that the former is purely unselfish, and the man who feels it is totally unconcerned as to what the result of his devotion may be as regards himself, while the latter is always aroused by the hope and desire of gaining some advantage through it; so that on the second astral sub-plane such religious feeling as is there active invariably contains an element of selfish bargaining, while the devotion which raises a man to this sixth devachanic sub-plane is entirely free from any such taint.

On the other hand this phase of devotion, which consists essentially in the perpetual adoration of a personal deity, must be carefully distinguished from those still higher forms which find their expression in performing some definite work for the deity's sake. A few examples of the cases observed on this sub-plane will perhaps show these distinctions more clearly than any mere description can do.

A fairly large number of entities whose devachanic activities work themselves out on this level are drawn from the oriental religions; but only those are included who have the characteristic of pure but comparatively unreasoning and unintelligent devotion. Worshippers of Vishnu, both in his avatâr of Krishna and otherwise, as well as a few followers of Shiva, are to be found here, each wrapped up in the self-woven cocoon of his own thoughts, alone with his own god, and oblivious of the rest

24

of mankind, except in so far as his affections may associate with him in his adoration those whom he loved on earth. A Vaishnavite, for example, was noticed wholly absorbed in the ecstatic worship of the very same image of Vishnu to which he had made offerings during life.

Some of the most characteristic examples of this plane are to be found among women, who indeed form a very large majority of its inhabitants. Among others there was a Hindu woman who had glorified her husband into a divine being, and also thought of the child Krishna as playing with her own children, but while these latter were thoroughly human and real the child Krishna was obviously nothing but the semblance of a blue wooden image galvanized into life. Krishna also appeared in her Devachan under another form—that of an effeminate young man playing on a flute; but she was not in the least confused or troubled by this double manifestation. Another woman, who was a worshipper of Shiva, had confounded the god with her husband, looking upon the latter as a manifestation of the former, so that the one seemed to be constantly changing into the other. Some Buddhists also are found upon this subdivision, but apparently exclusively those who regard the Buddha rather as an object of adoration than as a great teacher.

The Christian religion also contributes many of the inhabitants of this plane. The unintellectual devotion which is exemplified on the one hand by the illiterate Roman Catholic peasant, and on the other by the earnest and sincere "soldier" of the Salvation Army, seems to produce results very similar to those already described, for these people also are found wrapped up in contemplation of their ideas of Christ or his mother respectively. For instance, an Irish peasant was seen absorbed in the deepest adoration of the Virgin Mary, whom he imaged as standing on the moon after the fashion of Titian's "Assumption," but holding out her hands and' speaking to him. A mediæval monk was found in ecstatic contemplation of Christ crucified, and the intensity of his yearning love and pity was such that as he watched the blood dropping from the wounds of the figure of his Christ the stigmata reproduced themselves upon his own body.

Another man seemed to have forgotten the sad story of the crucifixion, and thought of his Christ only as glorified on his throne, with the crystal sea before him, and all around a vast multitude of worshippers, among whom he himself stood with his wife and family. His affection for these relatives was very deep, yet his thoughts were more occupied in adoration of the Christ, though his conception of his deity was so material that he imaged him as constantly changing kaleidoscopically backwards and forwards between the form of a man and that of the lamb bearing the flag which we often see represented in church windows.

A more interesting case was that of a Spanish nun who had died at about the age of nineteen or twenty. In her Devachan she carried herself back to the date of Christ's life upon earth, and imagined herself as accompanying him through the chain of events recounted in the gospels, and after his crucifixion taking care of his mother the Virgin Mary. Not unnaturally, perhaps, her pictures of the scenery and costumes of Palestine were entirely inaccurate, for the Saviour and his disciples wore the dress of Spanish peasants, while the hills round Jerusalem were mighty mountains clothed with vineyards, and the olive trees were hung with grey Spanish moss. She thought of herself as eventually martyred for her faith, and ascending into heaven, but yet only to live over and over again this life in which she so delighted.

A quaint and pretty little example of the Devachan of a child may conclude our list of instances from this sub-plane. He had died at the age of seven, and was occupied in re-enacting in the heaven-world the religious stories which his Irish nurse had told him down here; and best of all he loved to think of himself as playing with the infant Jesus, and helping him to make those clay sparrows which the power of the child-Christ is fabled to have brought to life and caused to fly.

It will be seen that the blind unreasoning devotion of which we have been speaking does not at any time raise its votaries to any great spiritual heights; but it must be remembered that in all cases they are entirely happy and most fully satisfied, for what they receive is always the highest which they are capable of appreciating. Nor is it without a very good effect on their future career, for although no amount of mere devotion such as this will ever develope intellect, yet it does produce an increased capacity for a higher form of devotion, and in most cases it leads also to purity of life. A person therefore who lives such a life and enjoys such a Devachan as we have been describing, though he is not likely to make rapid progress on the path of spiritual development, is at least guarded from many dangers, for it is very improbable that in his next birth he should fall into any of the grosser sins, or be drawn away from his devotional aspirations into a mere worldly life of avarice, ambition or dissipation. Nevertheless, a survey of this sub-plane distinctly emphasizes the necessity of following St. Peter's advice, "Add to your faith virtue, and to virtue *knowledge.*"

FIFTH SUB-PLANE.

The chief characteristic of this subdivision may be defined as devotion expressing itself in active work. The Christian on this plane, for example, instead of merely adoring his Saviour, would think of himself as going out into the world to work for him. It is especially the plane for the working out of great schemes and designs unrealized on earth—of great organizations inspired by religious devotion, and usually having for their object some philanthropic purpose. It must be borne in mind, however, that ever as we rise higher greater complexity and variety is introduced, so that though we may still be able to give a definite characteristic as on the whole dominating the plane, we shall yet be more and more liable to find variations and exceptions that do not so readily range themselves under the general heading.

A typical case, although somewhat above the average, was that of a man who was found working out a grand scheme for the amelioration of the condition of the lower classes. While a deeply religious man himself, he had felt that the first step necessary in dealing with the poor was to improve their physical condition; and the plan which he was now working out in Devachan, with triumphant success and loving attention to every detail, was one which had often crossed his mind while on earth, though he had been quite unable there to take any steps towards its realization.

His idea had been that, if possessed of enormous wealth, he would buy up and get into his own hands the whole of one of the smaller trades—one in which perhaps three or four large firms only were now engaged; and he thought that by so doing he could effect very large savings by doing away with competitive advertising and other wasteful forms of trade rivalry, and thus be able, while supplying goods to the public at the same price as now, to pay much better wages to his workmen. It was part of his scheme to buy a plot of land and erect upon it cottages for his workmen, each surrounded by its little garden; and after a certain number of years' service, each

26

workman was to acquire a share in the profits of the business which would be sufficient to provide for him in his old age. By working out this system the devachanee had hoped to show to the world that there was an eminently practical side to Christianity, and also to win the souls of his men to his own faith out of gratitude for the material benefits they had received.

Another not dissimilar case was that of an Indian prince whose ideal on earth had been the divine hero-king, Râma, on whose example he had tried to model his life and methods of government. Naturally down here all sorts of untoward accidents had occurred, and many of his schemes had consequently failed, but in Devachan everything went well, and the greatest possible result followed every one of his well-meant efforts—Râma of course personally advising and directing his work, and receiving perpetual adoration from all his devoted subjects.

A curious and rather touching instance of personal religious work was that of a woman who had been a nun, belonging to one not of the contemplative but of the working orders. She had evidently based her life upon the text "Inasmuch as ye have done it unto one of the least of these my brethren, ye have done it unto me," and now in Devachan she was still carrying out to the fullest extent the injunctions of her Lord, and was constantly occupied in healing the sick, in feeding the hungry, and clothing and helping the poor—the peculiarity of the case being that each of those to whom she had ministered at once changed into the appearance of the Christ, whom she then worshipped with fervent devotion.

An instructive case was that of two sisters, both of whom had been intensely religious; one of them had been a crippled invalid, and the other had spent a long life in tending her. On earth they had often discussed and planned what religious and philanthropic work they would carry out if they were able, and now each is the most prominent figure in the other's Devachan, the cripple being well and strong, while each thinks of the other as joining her in carrying out the unrealized wishes of her earth-life; and in this case the image of each sister in the other's Devachan was at least to some extent vivified and real.

On this plane also the higher type of sincere and devoted missionary activity finds expression. Of course the ordinary ignorant fanatic never reaches this level, but a few of the noblest cases, such as Livingstone, might be found here engaged in the congenial occupation of converting multitudes of people to the particular religion which they happened to advocate. One of the most striking of such cases which came under notice was that of a Mohammedan, who imagined himself as working most zealously at the conversion of the world and its government according to the most approved principles of the faith of Islam.

It appears that under certain conditions artistic capacity may also bring its votaries to this sub-plane. But here a careful distinction must be drawn. The artist or musician whose only object is the selfish one of personal fame, or who habitually allows himself to be influenced by feelings of professional jealousy, of course generates no forces which will bring him to the devachanic plane at all. On the other hand that grandest type of art whose disciples regard it as a mighty power entrusted to them for the spiritual elevation of their fellows will express itself in even higher regions than this. But between these two extremes those devotees of art who follow it for its own sake or regard it as an offering to their deity, never thinking of its effect on their fellows, may in some cases find their appropriate Devachan on this sub-plane.

As an example of this may be mentioned a musician of very religious temperament who regarded all his labour of love simply as an offering to the Christ, and knew nothing of the magnificent arrangement of sound and colour which his soul-inspiring compositions were producing in the matter of the devachanic plane. Nor would all his enthusiasm be wasted and fruitless, for its result would certainly be to give him increased devotion and increased musical capacity in his next birth; but without the still wider aspiration to help humanity this kind of Devachan might repeat itself almost indefinitely. Indeed, glancing back at the three planes with which we have just been dealing we may notice that they are in all cases concerned with the working out of devotion to personalities—either to one's family and friends or to a personal deity—rather than the wider devotion to humanity for its own sake which finds its expression on the next sub-plane.

FOURTH SUB-PLANE.

So varied are the activities of this, the highest of the rûpa levels, that it is difficult to group them under a single characteristic. Perhaps they might best be arranged into four main divisions—unselfish pursuit of spiritual knowledge, high philosophic or scientific thought, literary or artistic ability exercised for unselfish purposes, and service for service's sake. The exact definition of each of these classes will be more readily comprehended when some examples of each have been given.

Naturally it is from those religions in which the necessity of obtaining spiritual knowledge is recognized that most of the population of this sub-plane is drawn. It will be remembered that on the sixth sub-plane we found many Buddhists whose religion had chiefly taken the form of devotion to their great leader as a person; here on the contrary we have those more intelligent followers whose supreme aspiration was to sit at his feet and learn—who looked upon him in the light of a teacher rather than as a being to be adored.

Now in their Devachan this highest wish is fulfilled; they find themselves in very truth learning from the Buddha, and the image which they have thus made of him is no mere empty form, but most assuredly has in it a ray which is really part of himself. They are therefore beyond doubt acquiring fresh knowledge and wider views; and the effect upon their next life cannot but be of the most marked character. They will not, of course, remember any individual facts that they may have learnt (though when such facts are presented to their minds in a subsequent life they will grasp them with avidity and intuitively recognize their truth), but the result of the teaching will be to build into the ego a strong tendency to take broader and more philosophical views on all such subjects. Thus it will be seen that the Devachan enjoyed on this higher subdivision very definitely and unmistakably hastens the evolution of the ego; and once more our attention is drawn to the enormous advantage gained by those who have in their Devachan the figures of real, living and powerful teachers.

A less developed type of this form of instruction is found in cases in which some really great and spiritual writer has become to a student a living personality, and has taken on the aspect of a friend, forming part of the student's mental life—an ideal figure in his musings. Such an one may enter into the pupil's Devachan, and by virtue of his own highly evolved ego may vivify the devachanic image of himself, and further illuminate the teachings in his own books, bringing out of them the more hidden meanings.

Many of the followers of the path of wisdom among the Hindus find their Devachan upon this plane—that is, if their Gurus have been men possessing any real knowledge. A few of the more advanced among the Sûfîs and Parsîs are also here, and we still find some of the early Gnostics whose spiritual development was such as to earn for them a prolonged stay in this celestial region. But except for this comparatively small number of Sûfîs and Gnostics neither Mohammedanism nor Christianity seems to raise its followers to this level, though of course some who nominally belong to these religions may be carried on to this sub-plane by the presence in their character of qualities which do not depend upon the teachings peculiar to their religion.

In this region we also find earnest and devoted students of Occultism who are not yet so far advanced as to have earned the right and the power to forego their Devachan for the good of the world. Among these was one who in life had been personally known to some of the investigators—a Buddhist monk who had been an earnest student of Theosophy, and had long cherished the hope of being one day privileged to receive instruction directly from its adept teachers. In his Devachan the Buddha was the dominant figure, while the two Masters who have been most closely concerned with the Theosophical Society appeared also as his lieutenants, expounding and illustrating his teaching. All three of these images were very fully vitalized and informed by the power and wisdom of the great beings whom they represented, and the monk was therefore definitely receiving real teaching upon occult subjects, the effect of which would almost certainly be to bring him actually on to the Path of Initiation in his next birth.

Another instance from our ranks which was encountered on this level illustrates the terrible effect of harbouring unfounded and uncharitable suspicions. It was the case of a devoted and self-sacrificing student who towards the end of her life had unfortunately fallen into an attitude of quite unworthy and unjustifiable distrust of the motives of her old friend and teacher, Madame Blavatsky; and it was sad to notice how this feeling had shut out to a considerable extent the higher influence and teaching which she might have enjoyed in her Devachan. It was not that the influence and teaching were in any way withheld from her, but that her own mental attitude rendered her to some extent unreceptive of them. She was of course quite unconscious of this, and seemed to herself to be enjoying the fullest and most perfect communion with the Masters, yet it was obvious to the investigators that but for this unfortunate self-limitation she would have reaped far greater advantage from her stay on this level.

It will be understood that since there are other Masters of wisdom besides those connected with our own movement, and other schools of occultism working along the same general lines as that to which they belong, students attached to some of these are also frequently met with upon this sub-plane.

Passing now to the next class, that of high philosophic and scientific thought, we find here many of those nobler and more unselfish thinkers who seek insight and knowledge only for the purpose of enlightening and helping their fellows. We are of course not including as students of philosophy those men, either in the east or the west, who waste their time in mere verbal argument and hair-splitting—a form of discussion which has its roots in selfishness and conceit, and can therefore never help towards a real understanding of the facts of the universe; for naturally such foolish superficiality as this produces no results that can work themselves out on the devachanic plane.

As an instance of a true student noticed on this sub-plane we may mention one of the later followers of the neo-platonic system, whose name has fortunately been preserved to us in the surviving records of that period. He had striven all through his earth-life really to master the teachings of that school, and now his Devachan was occupied in unravelling its mysteries and in endeavouring to understand its bearing upon human life and development.

Another case was that of an astronomer, who seemed to have begun life as a Christian, but had gradually under the influence of his studies widened out into Pantheism; in his Devachan he was still pursuing these studies with a mind full of reverence, and was undoubtedly gaining real knowledge, apparently from the Devas who are concerned on this plane with the distribution and administration of stellar influences. He was lost in contemplation of a vast panorama of whirling nebulae and gradually-forming systems and worlds, and he appeared to be groping after some dim idea as to the shape of the universe, which he imagined as some vast animal. His thoughts surrounded him as elemental forms shaped as stars, and one especial source of joy to him consisted in listening to the stately rhythm of the music that pealed out in mighty chorales from the moving orbs.

The third type of activity on this plane is that highest kind of artistic and literary effort which is chiefly inspired by a desire to elevate and spiritualize the race. Here we find all our greatest musicians; on this sub-plane Mozart, Beethoven, Bach, Wagner and others are still flooding the heaven-world with harmony far more glorious even than the grandest which they were able to produce when on earth. It seems as if a great stream of divine music poured into them from higher regions, and was, as it were, specialized by them and made their own, to be then sent forth through all the plane in a great tide of melody which adds to the bliss of all around. Those who are functioning in full consciousness on the devachanic plane will clearly hear and thoroughly appreciate this magnificent outpouring, but even the disembodied entities of this level, each of whom is wrapped up in his own thought-cloud, are affected also by the elevating and ennobling influence of its resonant melody.

The painter and the sculptor also, if they have followed their respective arts always with a grand, unselfish aim, are here constantly making and sending forth all kinds of lovely forms for the delight and encouragement of their fellow-men—the forms being, of course, artificial elementals created by their thought. And not only may these beautiful conceptions give pleasure to those living entirely upon this plane; they may also in many cases be grasped by the minds of artists still in the flesh—may act as inspirations to them, and so be reproduced down here for the elevating and ennobling of that portion of humanity which is struggling amid the turmoil of physical life.

One touching and beautiful figure seen upon this plane was that of a boy who had been a chorister, and had died at the age of fourteen. His whole soul was full of music and of boyish devotion to his art, deeply coloured with the thought that by it he was expressing the religious longings of the multitude who crowded a vast cathedral, and yet was at the same time pouring out to them celestial encouragement and inspiration. He had known little enough save for this one great gift of song, but he had used that gift worthily, trying to he the voice of the people to heaven and of heaven to the people, and ever longing to know more music and render it more worthily for the Church's sake. In his Devachan his wish was bearing fruit, and over him was bending a teacher in a form evidently made by his mind from the quaint angular figure of a mediæval St. Cecilia in a stained glass window, and this thought-image was vivified by a Deva, who through it taught him greater music than he had ever dreamed on earth.

Here also was one of earth's failures—for the tragedy of the earth-life leaves strange marks sometimes even in "the heavenly places." He was alone in Devachan; in the world where all thoughts of loved ones smile upon man as friends, he was thinking and writing in solitude. On earth he had striven to write a great book, and for the sake of it had refused to use his literary power in making mere sustenance from paltry hack-work; but none would look at his book, and he walked the streets despairing, till sorrow and starvation closed his eyes to earth. He had been lonely all his life—in his youth friendless and shut out from family ties, and in his manhood able to work only in his own way, pushing aside hands that would have led him to a wider view of life's possibilities than the earthly paradise which he longed to make for all. Now, as he thought and wrote, though there were none he had loved as personal or ideal helpers who could make part of his devachanic life, he saw stretching before him the Utopia of which he had dreamed, for which he had tried to live, and the vast thronging impersonal multitudes whom he had longed to serve; and the joy of their joy surged back on him and made his solitude a heaven. When he is born again to earth he will surely return with power to achieve as well as to plan, and the devachanic vision will be partially bodied forth in happier terrene lives.

Many were found on this plane who during their earth-stay had devoted themselves to helping men because they felt the tie of brotherhood—who rendered service for service's sake rather than because they desired to please any particular deity. They were engaged in working out with full knowledge and calm wisdom vast schemes of beneficence, magnificent plans of world-improvement, and at the same time they were maturing powers with which to carry them out hereafter on the lower plane of physical life.

THE ARÛPA LEVELS.

We now pass from the four lower or rûpa levels of Devachan, on which the personality functions, to the three higher or arûpa levels, where the reincarnating ego has his home. Here, so far as he sees at all, he sees clearly, for he has risen above the illusions of personality and the refracting medium of the lower self, and though his consciousness may be dim, dreamily unobservant and scarcely awake, yet his vision is at least true, however limited. The conditions of consciousness are so far away from all with which we are familiar down here that all terms known to psychology are useless and misleading. This has been called the realm of the noumenal in contrast with the phenomenal, of the formless in contrast with the formed; but it is still a world of manifestation, however real when opposed to the unrealities of lower states, and it still has forms, however rare in their materials and subtle in their essence.

THIRD SUB-PLANE.

This, the lowest of the arûpa sub-planes, is also by far the most populous of all the regions with which we are acquainted, for here are present almost all the sixty thousand millions of egos who are said to be engaged in the present human evolution—all, in fact, except the comparatively small number who are capable of functioning on the second and first sub-planes. Each ego is represented by an ovoid form, the auric egg—at first a mere film, colourless and almost invisible, of most tenuous consistency; but, as the ego developes, this body begins to show a shimmering iridescence like a soap-bubble, colours playing over its surface like the changing hues made by sunlight on the spray of a waterfall. Composed of matter inconceivably fine, delicate and ethereal, intensely alive and pulsating with living fire, it becomes as its evolution proceeds a radiant globe of flashing colours, its high vibrations sending ripples of changing hues over its surface—hues of which earth knows nothing—brilliant, soft and luminous beyond the power of language to describe. Take the colours of an Egyptian sunset and add to them the wonderful softness of an English sky at eventide—raise these as high above themselves in light and translucency and splendour as they are above the colours given by the cakes of a child's paint-box—and even then none who have not seen can image the beauty of these radiant orbs which flash into the field of the devachanic sight as it is lifted to the vision of this supernal world.

All these causal bodies are filled with living fire drawn from a higher plane, with which the globe appears to be connected by a quivering thread of intense light, vividly recalling to the mind the words of the Stanzas of Dzyân, "the Spark hangs from the Flame by the finest thread of Fohat;" and as the ego grows and is able to receive more and more from the inexhaustible ocean of Âtmâ-Buddhi which pours down through the thread as a channel, the latter expands and gives wider passage to the flood, till on the next sub-plane it might he imaged as a water-spout connecting earth and sky, and higher still as itself a great globe through which rushes the living spring, until the causal body seems to melt into the inpouring light. Once more the Stanza says it for us: "The thread between the Watcher and his shadow becomes more strong and radiant with every change. The morning sunlight has changed into noon-day glory. This is thy present wheel, said the Flame to the Spark. Thou art myself, my image and my shadow. I have clothed myself in thee, and thou art my vâhan to the day, 'Be-with-us, when thou shalt re-become myself and others, thyself and me."

The egos who are connected with a physical body are distinguishable from those enjoying the disembodied state by a difference in the types of vibrations set up on the surface of the globes, and it is therefore easy to see at a glance whether an individual is or is not in incarnation at the time. The immense majority, whether in or out of the body, are but dreamily semiconscious, though few are now in the condition of mere colourless films; those who are fully awake are marked and brilliant exceptions, standing out amid the less radiant crowds like stars of the first magnitude, and between these and the least-developed are ranged every variety of size and beauty of colour—each thus representing the exact stage of evolution at which it has arrived.

The majority are not yet sufficiently definite, even in such consciousness as they possess, to understand the purpose or the laws of the evolution in which they are engaged; they seek incarnation in obedience to the impulse of the Cosmic Will, and also to *Tanhâ*, the blind thirst for manifested life—a desire to find some region in which they can feel and be conscious of living; they put forth as groping, waving tentacles into the ocean of existence the personalities which are themselves on the lower planes of life, but they are as yet in no sense aware that these personalities are the means whereby they are to be nourished and to grow. They see nothing of their past or their future, not being yet conscious on their own plane. Still, as they are slowly drawing in experience and assimilating it, there grows up a sense that certain things are good to do and others bad, and this expresses itself imperfectly in the connected personality as the beginning of a conscience, a feeling of right and wrong: and gradually as they develope, this sense more and more clearly formulates itself in the lower nature, and becomes a less inefficient guide of conduct.

When the personality belonging to an ego in this undeveloped condition has completed its Devachan on the rûpa levels, it yields up to the higher individuality whatever it has assimilated and transmuted, itself disintegrating and leaving the ego as the sole survivor, the real and enduring man. But at that moment, before it puts itself forth again into embodied existence, the ego has a flash of consciousness, showing the results of the life that is completed, and something of what will follow from that life in the next; for a moment all that there is of the man is in the arûpa world, and thence it again descends. These glimpses may be said to be the opportunities of the ego. At first it makes little of them, being so dimly conscious and so poorly fitted to apprehend facts and their interrelations; but gradually the power to appreciate what is seen increases, and later the ability comes to remember the flashes of the past and to compare them, and thus to mark out the road which is being traversed, and estimate the progress made and the direction in which it is going.

In this way the most advanced egos of this sub-plane develope to a point at which they are engaged in studying their past, tracing out the causes set going in it, and learning much from the retrospection, so that the impulses sent downwards become clearer and more definite, and translate themselves in the lower con-sciousness as firm convictions and imperative intuitions.

It is perhaps scarcely necessary to repeat that the thought-images of the rûpa levels are not carried into the arûpa world; if an ego conscious on this plane has been surrounded by the images of less developed individualities who were dear to him on earth, he comes into contact with them in this higher region as they really are, and will find them irresponsive to him here, because they have not yet developed their consciousness on this loftier plane. This, however, can be but an exceedingly rare case, and even when it occurs the ego experiences no sense of loss, for the ties that are only of the personality have no power over him; his true relations are with other individualities, and these endure when the personality vanishes, so that on the arûpa levels each ego knows his real kindred, sees them and is seen in his own royal nature, as the true immortal man that passes on from life to life, with all the ties intact that are knit to his real being.

SECOND SUB-PLANE.

From the densely-thronged region which we have been considering we pass into a more thinly-populated world, as out of a great city into a peaceful countryside; for at the present stage of human evolution only a small minority of individuals have risen to this loftier level where even the least advanced is definitely self-conscious, and also conscious of his surroundings. Able at least to some extent to review the past through which he has come, the ego on this level is aware of the purpose and method of evolution; he knows that he is engaged in a work of self-development, and recognizes the stages of physical and *post-mortem* life through which he passes in his lower vehicles. The personality with which he is connected is seen by him as part of himself, and he endeavours to guide it, using his knowledge of the past as a store of experience from which he formulates principles of conduct, clear and immutable convictions of right and wrong. These he sends down into his lower mind, super-intending and directing its activities. While he continually fails in the earlier part of his life on this sub-plane to make the lower mind understand logically the foundations of the principles he impresses on it, he yet very definitely succeeds in making the impression, and such abstract ideas as truth, justice and honour become unchallenged and ruling conceptions in the lower mental life.

There are rules of conduct enforced by social, national and religious sanctions, by which a man guides himself in daily life, and yet which may be swept away by some rush of temptation, some overmastering surge of passion and desire; but there are some things an evolved man *cannot* do—things which are against his very nature; he cannot lie, or betray, or do a dishonourable action. Into the inmost fibres of his being certain principles are wrought, and to act against them is an impossibility, no matter what may be the strain of circumstance or the torrent of temptation; for these things are of the life of the ego. While, however, he thus succeeds in guiding his lower vehicle, his knowledge of it and its doings is often far from precise and clear. He sees the lower planes but dimly, understanding their principles rather than their details, and part of his evolution on this plane consists of coming more and more consciously into direct touch with the personality which so imperfectly represents him below.

It will he understood from this that only such egos as are deliberately aiming at spiritual growth live on this plane, and they have in consequence become largely receptive of influences from the planes above them. The channel of communication grows and enlarges, and a fuller flood pours through. The thought under this influence takes on a singularly clear and piercing quality, even in the less developed, and the effect of this in the lower mind shows itself as a tendency to philosophic and abstract thinking. In the more highly evolved the vision is far-reaching: it ranges with clear insight over the past, recognizing the causes set up, their working out, and what remains still unexhausted of their effects.

The egos living on this plane have wide opportunities for growth when freed from the physical body, for here they may receive instructions from more advanced entities, coming into direct touch with their teachers. No longer by thought-pictures, but by a flashing luminousness impossible to describe, the very essence of the idea flies like a star from one ego to the other, its correlations expressing themselves as light waves pouring out from the central star, and needing no separate enunciation. A thought is like a light placed in a room; it shows all things round it, but requires no words to describe them.

First Sub-Plane.

This, the most glorious level of the devachanic world, has but few denizens from our humanity, for none but Masters and initiates dwell on its heights. Of the beauty of form and colour and sound here no words can speak, for mortal language has no terms in which those radiant splendours may find expression. Enough that they *are,* and that some of our race are wearing them, the earnest of what others shall be, the fruition of which the seed was sown on lowlier planes. These have accomplished the mânasic evolution, and have unified self-consciousness; from their eyes the illusion-veil of personality has been lifted, and they know and realize that they are not the lower nature, but only use it as a vehicle of experience. It may still have power in the less evolved of them to shackle and to hamper, but they can never fall into the blunder of confusing it with themselves. From this they are saved by carrying their consciousness through unbroken, not only from day to day but from life to life, so that past lives are not so much looked back upon as always present in the consciousness, the man feeling them as one life rather than as many.

From this highest level of the arûpa world come down most of the influences poured out by the Masters as they work for the evolution of the human race, acting on the individualities of men, shedding on them the inspiring energies which stimulate spiritual growth, which enlighten the intellect and purify the emotions. Hence genius receives its illumination; here all upward efforts find their guidance. As the sun-rays fall everywhere from one centre, and each body that receives them uses them after its nature, so from the Elder Brothers of the race fall on all egos the light and life which it is their function to dispense; and each uses as much as it can assimilate, and thereby grows and evolves. Thus, as everywhere else, the highest glory of the devachanic world is found in the glory of service, and they who have accomplished the mânasic evolution are the fountains from which flows strength for those who still are climbing.

II. NON-HUMAN.

When we attempt to describe the non-human inhabitants of the devachanic plane, we at once find ourselves face to face with difficulties of the most insuperable character. For in touching the arûpa levels we come into contact for the first time with a plane which is cosmic in its extent—on which therefore may be met many an entity which mere human language has no words to portray. For the purposes of our present paper it will probably be best to put aside altogether those vast hosts of beings whose range is cosmic, and confine our remarks strictly to the inhabitants peculiar to the mânasic plane of our own chain of worlds. It may be remembered that in the manual on *The Astral Plane* the same course was adopted, no attempt being made to describe visitors from other planets and systems; and although such visitors as were there only occasional would here be very much more frequent, it is obviously desirable in an essay for general reading to adhere to the same rule. A few words, therefore, upon the elemental essence of the plane and the sections of the great Deva kingdom which are especially connected with it will be as much as it will be useful to give here; and the extreme difficulty of presenting even these comparatively simple ideas will conclusively show how impossible it would be to deal with others which could not but be far more complicated.

THE ELEMENTAL ESSENCE.

It may be remembered that in one of the earlier letters received from an Adept teacher the remark was made that to comprehend the condition of the first and second of the elemental kingdoms was impossible except to an initiate—an observation which shows how partial must be the success which can attend any effort to describe them down here upon the physical plane. It will be well first of all that we should endeavour to form as clear an idea in our minds as possible of what elemental essence really is, since this is a point upon which much confusion often seems to exist, even amongst those who have made considerable study of

35

Theosophical literature.

WHAT IT IS.

Elemental essence, then, is merely a name applied during certain early stages of its evolution to monadic essence, which in its turn may be defined as the outpouring of Âtmâ-Buddhi into matter. We are all familiar with the fact that before this outpouring arrives at the stage of individualization at which it ensouls a man, it has passed through and ensouled in turn six lower phases of evolution—the animal, vegetable, mineral and three elemental kingdoms. When energizing through those respective stages it has sometimes been called the animal, vegetable or mineral monad—though this term is distinctly misleading, since long before it arrives at any of these kingdoms it has become not *one* but *many* monads. The name was however adopted to convey the idea that, though differentiation in the monadic essence had already long ago set in, it had not yet been carried to the extent of individualization. Now when this monadic essence is energizing through the three great elemental kingdoms which precede the mineral it is called by the name of "elemental essence."

THE VEILING OF ÂTMÂ.

Before, however, its nature and the manner in which it manifests itself on the various planes can be understood, the method in which Âtmâ enfolds itself in its descent into matter must be realized. We are not now dealing with the original formation of the matter of the planes by aggregation after a universal pralaya, but simply with the descent of a new wave of evolution into matter already existing.

Before the period of which we are speaking, this wave of life has spent countless ages evolving, in a manner of which we can have very little comprehension, through the successive encasements of atoms, molecules and cells: but we will leave all that earlier part of its stupendous history out of account for the moment, and consider only its descent into the matter of planes somewhat more within the grasp of human intellect, though still far above the merely physical level.

Be it understood then that when Âtmâ, resting on any plane (it matters not which), on its path downward into matter, is driven by the resistless force of its own evolution to pass onward to the plane next below, it must, in order to manifest itself there, enfold itself in the matter of that lower plane—draw round itself as a body a veil of that matter, to which it will act as soul or energizing force. Similarly, when it continues its descent to a third plane, it must draw round itself some of *its* matter, and we shall have then an entity whose body or outer covering consists of the matter of that third plane.

But the force energizing in it—its soul, so to speak—will not be Âtmâ in the condition in which it was upon the higher plane on which we first found it; it will be that Âtmâ *plus* the veil of the matter of the second plane through which it has passed. When a still further descent is made to a fourth plane, the entity becomes still more complex, for it will then have a body of the matter of that fourth plane, ensouled by Âtmâ already twice veiled, in the matter of the second and third planes. It will be seen that, since this process repeats itself for every sub-plane of each plane of the solar system, by the time the original force reaches our physical level it is so thoroughly veiled that it is small wonder that men often fail to recognize it as Âtmâ at all.

Now suppose that the monadic essence has carried on this process of veiling itself down to the atomic level of the devachanic plane, and that, instead of descending through the various subdivisions of that plane, it plunges down directly into the astral plane, ensouling or aggregating around it a body of atomic astral matter; such a combination would be the elemental essence of the astral plane, belonging to the third of the great elemental kingdoms—the one immediately preceding the mineral. In the course of its two thousand four hundred differentiations on the astral plane it draws to itself many and various combinations of the matter of its several subdivisions; but these are only temporary, and it still remains essentially one kingdom, whose characteristic is monadic essence involved down to the atomic level of the devachanic plane only, but manifesting primarily through the atomic matter of the astral plane.

The elemental essence which we find on the devachanic plane constitutes the first and second of the great elemental kingdoms, but the principle of its formation is the same as that described above. A mass of monadic essence (the expression is materialistic and misleading, but it is difficult to see how to avoid it) carries on the process of veiling itself down to the atomic level of the buddhic plane, and then plunges down directly into the devachanic plane, ensouling a body of atomic devachanic matter—that is, of the matter belonging to the highest of the arûpa levels—and so becomes the elemental essence of the first great kingdom. In this—its simplest or natural condition, be it understood—it does not combine the atoms of the plane into molecules in order to form a body for itself, but simply applies by its attraction an immense compressing force to them. In the course of its differentiations it aggregates around itself various combinations of the matter of the second and third sub-divisions, but it never loses the special and definite characteristics which mark it as the elemental essence of the arûpa levels.

The second great kingdom, whose habitat is the rûpa division of Devachan, is formed upon a very similar principle. The essence of the first kingdom, after evolving through various differentiations during ages whose length is unknown to us, returns to its simplest condition—not of course, as it was before that evolution, but bearing within it all that it has gained throughout its course; and it then puts itself down directly into the fourth sub-division of Devachan—the highest of the rûpa levels—drawing to itself as a body some of the matter of that sub-plane. That is the simplest condition of the elemental essence of the second kingdom, but as before, it takes on in the course of its evolution garbs many and various, composed of combinations of the matter of the lower sub-planes.

It might naturally be supposed that these elemental kingdoms which exist and function upon the devachanic plane must certainly, being so much higher, be further advanced in evolution than the third kingdom, which belongs exclusively to the astral plane. This however is not so; for it must be remembered that in speaking of this phase of evolution the word "higher" means not, as usual, more advanced, but *less* advanced, since here we are dealing with the monadic essence on the downward sweep of its arc, and progress for the elemental essence therefore means descent into matter instead of, as with us, ascent towards higher planes. Unless the student bears this fact constantly and clearly in mind, he will again and again find himself beset by perplexing anomalies, and his view of this side of evolution will be lacking in grasp and comprehensiveness.

The general characteristics of elemental essence were indicated at considerable length in the manual on *The Astral Plane,* and all that is there said as to the number of subdivisions in the kingdoms and their marvellous impressibility by human thought is equally true of these devachanic varieties. A few words should perhaps be said to explain how the seven horizontal subdivisions of each kingdom arrange themselves in connection with the sub-planes of Devachan. In the case of the first kingdom, its highest subdivision corresponds with the first sub-plane of Devachan, while the second and third sub-planes are each divided into three parts, each of which is the habitat of one of the elemental subdivisions. The second kingdom distributes itself over the rûpa levels, its highest subdivision corresponding to the fourth sub-plane, while the fifth, sixth and seventh sub-planes are each divided into two to accommodate the remainder.

HOW THE ESSENCE EVOLVES.

So much was written in the earlier part of this manual as to the effect of thought upon the devachanic elemental essence that it will be unnecessary to return to that branch of the subject now; but it must be borne in mind that it is, if possible, even more instantaneously sensitive to thought-action here than it is on the astral plane, the wonderful delicacy with which it responds to the faintest action of the mind being constantly and prominently brought before our investigators. We shall grasp this capability the more fully if we realize that it is in such response that its very life consists—that its progress is due to the use made of it in the process of thought by the more advanced entities whose evolution it shares.

If it could be imagined as entirely free for a moment from the action of thought, it would be but a formless conglomeration of dancing infinitesimal atoms—instinct indeed with a marvellous intensity of life, yet making no kind of progress on the downward path of its involution into matter. But when by the thoughts of the beings functioning on those respective planes it is thrown on the rûpa levels into all kinds of lovely forms, and on the arûpa levels into flashing streams, it receives a distinct additional impulse which, often repeated, helps it forward on its way. For whenever a thought is directed from those higher levels to the affairs of earth, it naturally sweeps downward and takes upon itself the matter of the lower planes. In doing so it brings into contact with that matter the elemental essence of which its first veil was formed, and so by degrees habituates it to answering to lower vibrations; thus, very gradually, proceeds its downward evolution into matter.

Very noticeably also is it affected by music—by the splendid floods of glorious sound of which we have previously spoken as poured forth upon these lofty planes by the great masters of melody who are carrying on there in far fuller measure the work which down here on this dull earth they had only commenced.

Another point which should be remembered is the vast difference between the grandeur and power of thought on this plane and the comparative feebleness of the efforts that we dignify with that name down here. Our ordinary thought begins in the mind-body on the rûpa levels and clothes itself as it descends with the appropriate astral elemental essence; but when a man has advanced so far as to have his consciousness active in the true ego upon the arûpa levels, then his thought commences there and clothes itself first in the elemental essence of the rûpa levels, and is consequently infinitely finer, more penetrating and in every way more effective. If the thought be directed exclusively to higher objects, its vibrations may be of too fine a character to find expression on the astral plane at all; but when they do affect this lower matter they will do so with much more far-reaching effect than those which are generated so much nearer to its own level.

Following this idea a stage further we see the thought of the initiate taking its rise upon the buddhic plane, above Devachan altogether, and clothing itself with the elemental essence of the arûpa levels for garment, while the thought of the Adept pours down from Nirvana itself, wielding the tremendous, the wholly incalculable powers of regions beyond the ken of mere ordinary humanity. Thus ever as our conceptions rise higher we see before us wider and wider fields of usefulness for our enormously increased capacities, and we realize how true is the saying that the work of one day on levels such as these may well surpass in efficiency the toil of a thousand years on the physical plane.

THE DEVAS.

So much of the little that can be expressed in human language about these wonderful and exalted beings was written in *The Astral Plane* that it is unnecessary to go at length into the subject here. For the information of those who have not that manual at hand I will repeat here somewhat of the general explanation there given with reference to these entities.

The highest system of evolution connected with this earth, so far as we know, is that of the beings whom Hindus call the Devas, and who have elsewhere been spoken of as angels, sons of God, etc. They may in fact be regarded as a kingdom lying next above humanity in the same way as humanity in turn lies next above the animal kingdom, but with this important difference, that while for an animal there is no possibility of evolution through any kingdom but the human, man, when he attains the level of the Asekha, or full Adept, finds various paths of advancement opening before him, of which this great Deva evolution is only one (see article on "The Steps of the Path," in *Lucifer* for October, 1896).

In Oriental literature this word "Deva" is frequently used vaguely to mean almost any kind of non-human entity, so that it would often include DHYÂN CHOHANS on the one hand and nature-spirits and artificial elementals on the other. Here, however, its use will be restricted to the magnificent evolution which we are now considering.

Though connected with this earth, the Devas are by no means confined to it, for the whole of our present chain of seven worlds is as one world to them, their evolution being through a grand system of seven chains. Their hosts have hitherto been recruited chiefly from other humanities in the solar system, some lower and some higher than ours, since but a very small portion of our own has as yet reached the level at which for us it is possible to join them: but it seems certain that some of their very numerous classes have not passed in their upward progress through any humanity at all comparable with ours.

It is not possible for us at present to understand very much about them, but it is clear that what may be described as the aim of their evolution is considerably higher than ours; that is to say, while the object of our human evolution is to raise the successful portion of humanity to the position of the Asekha Adept by the end of the seventh round, the object of the Deva evolution is to raise their foremost rank to a very much higher level in the corresponding period. For them, as for us, a steeper but shorter path to still more sublime heights lies open to earnest endeavour; but what those heights may be in their case we can only conjecture.

Their three lower great divisions, beginning from the bottom, are generally called Kâmadevas, Rûpadevas, and Arûpadevas respectively. Just as our ordinary body here—the lowest body possible for us—is the physical, so the ordinary body of a Kâmadeva is the astral; so that he stands in somewhat the same position as humanity will do when it reaches planet F, and he, living ordinarily in an astral body, would go out of it to higher spheres in a Mâyâvirûpa just as we might in an astral body, while to enter the causal body would be to him (when sufficiently developed) no greater effort than to form a Mâyâvirûpa might be to us. In the same way the Rûpadeva's ordinary body would be the Mâyâvirûpa, since his habitat is the four rapa levels of the devachanic plane; while the Arûpadeva belongs to the three higher levels of that plane, and owns no nearer approach to a body than the Kârana Sharîra. Above the Arûpadevas there are four other great classes of this kingdom, inhabiting respectively the four higher planes of our solar system; and again above and beyond the Deva kingdom altogether stand the great hosts of the DHYÂN CHOHANS, but the consideration of such glorified beings would be out of place here.

Each of the two great divisions of this kingdom which have been mentioned as inhabiting the devachanic plane contains within itself many different classes; but their life is in every way so far removed from our own that it is useless to endeavour to give anything but the most general idea of it. I do not know that I can better indicate the impression produced upon the minds of our investigators on the subject than by reproducing the very words used by one of them at the time of the enquiry: "I get the effect of an intensely exalted consciousness—a consciousness glorious beyond all words; yet so very strange; so different—so entirely different from anything I have ever felt before, so unlike any possible kind of human experience, that it is absolutely hopeless to try to put it into words."

Equally hopeless is it on this physical plane to try to give any idea of the appearance of these mighty beings, for it changes with every line of thought which they follow. Some reference was made earlier in this paper to the magnificence and wonderful power of expression of their colour-language, and it will also have been realized from some passing remarks made in describing the human inhabitants that under certain conditions it is possible for men functioning upon this plane to learn much from them. It may be remembered how one of them had animated the angel-figure in the Devachan of a chorister, and was teaching him music grander far than any ever heard by earthly ears, and how in another case those connected with the wielding of certain planetary influences were helping forward the devachanic evolution of a certain astronomer.

Their relation to the nature-spirits (for an account of whom see Manual V.) might be described as somewhat resembling, though on a higher scale, that of men to the animal kingdom; for just as the animal can attain individualization only by association with man, so it appears that a permanent reincarnating individuality can normally be acquired by a nature-spirit only by an attachment of somewhat similar character to members of some of the orders of Devas.

Of course nothing that has been, or indeed can be, said of this great Deva evolution does more than brush the fringe of a very mighty subject, the fuller elaboration of which it must be left to each reader to make for himself when he develops the consciousness of these higher planes; yet what has been written, slight and unsatisfactory as it is and must be, may help to give some faint idea of the hosts of helpers with which man's advance in evolution will bring him into touch, and to show how every aspiration which his increased capacities make possible for him as he ascends is more than satisfied by the beneficent arrangements which nature has made for him.

III. ARTIFICIAL.

Very few words need be said upon this branch of our subject. The devachanic plane is even more fully peopled than the astral by the artificial elementals called into temporary existence by the thoughts of its inhabitants; and when it is remembered how much grander and more powerful thought is upon this plane, and that its forces are being wielded not only by the human inhabitants, embodied and disembodied, but by the Devas and by visitors from higher planes, it will at once be seen that the importance and influence of such artificial entities can hardly be exaggerated. It is not necessary here to go over again the ground traversed in the previous manual as to the effect of men's thoughts and the necessity of guarding them carefully; and enough was said in describing the difference between the action of thought on the rûpa and arûpa levels to show how the artificial elemental of the devachanic plane is called into existence, and to give some idea of the infinite variety of temporary entities which might be so produced, and the immense importance of the work that might be, and constantly is, done by their means. Great use is made of them by Adepts and initiates, and it is needless to say that the artificial elemental formed by such powerful minds as these is a being of infinitely longer existence and proportionately greater power than any of those described in dealing with the astral plane.

CONCLUSION.

In glancing over what has been written, the prominent idea is not unnaturally a humiliating sense of the utter inadequacy of all the attempts at description—of the hopelessness of any effort to put into human words the ineffable glories of the heaven-world. Still, lamentably imperfect as such an essay as this must he, it is yet better than nothing, and it may serve to put into the mind of the reader some faint conception of what awaits him on the other side of the grave; and though when he reaches this bright realm of bliss he will certainly find infinitely more than he has been led to expect, he will not, it is hoped, have to unlearn any of the information that he has here acquired.

Man, as at present constituted, has within him principles belonging to two planes even higher than Devachan, for his Buddhi represents him upon what from that very fact we call the buddhic plane, and his Attila upon that third plane of the solar system which has usually been spoken of as the nirvânic. In the average man these highest principles are as yet almost entirely undeveloped, and in any case the planes to which they belong are still more beyond the reach of all description than was Devachan. It must suffice to say that on the buddhic plane all limitations begin to fall away, and the consciousness of man expands until he realizes, no longer in theory only, but by absolute experience, that the consciousness of his fellows is included within his own, and he feels and knows and experiences with an absolute perfection of sympathy all that is in them, because it is in reality a part of himself; while on the nirvânic plane he moves a step further, and realizes that his consciousness and theirs are one in a yet higher sense, because they are all in reality facets of the infinitely greater consciousness of the Locos, in Whom they all live and move and have their being; so that when "the dewdrop slips into the shining sea" the effect produced is rather as though the process had been reversed and the ocean poured into the drop, which now for the first time realizes that it *is* the ocean—not a part of it, but the whole. Paradoxical, utterly incomprehensible, apparently impossible; yet absolutely true.

But this much at least we may grasp—that the blessed state of Nirvâna is not, as some have ignorantly supposed, a condition of blank nothingness, but of far more intense and beneficent activity; and that ever as we rise higher in the scale of nature our possibilities become greater, our work for others ever grander and more far-reaching, and that infinite wisdom and infinite power mean only infinite capacity for service, because they are directed by infinite love.

Printed in Great Britain
by Amazon